THE FINEST MUSIC

The Finest Music

Early Irish Lyrics

edited by

MAURICE RIORDAN

FABER & FABER

First published in 2014
by Faber & Faber Ltd
Bloomsbury House
74–77 Great Russell Street
London WC1B 3DA

This paperback edition first published in 2017

Typeset by RefineCatch Ltd, Bungay, Suffolk
Printed in England by Martins the Printers, Berwick-upon-Tweed

A CIP record for this book
is available from the British Library

ISBN 978-0-571-29802-0

2 4 6 8 10 9 7 5 3 1

In memory of Seamus Heaney

Once, as they rested on a chase, a debate arose among the Fianna-Finn as to what was the finest music in the world.

'Tell us that,' said Fionn, turning to Oisin.

'The cuckoo calling from the tree that is highest in the hedge,' cried his merry son.

'A good sound,' said Fionn. 'And you, Oscar,' he asked, 'what is to your mind the finest of music?'

'The top of music is the ring of a spear on a shield,' cried the stout lad.

'It is a good sound,' said Fionn.

And the other champions told their delight: the belling of a stag across water, the baying of a tuneful pack heard in the distance, the song of a lark, the laughter of a gleeful girl, or the whisper of a moved one.

'They are good sounds all,' said Fionn.

'Tell us, chief,' one ventured, 'what do you think?'

'The music of what happens,' said great Fionn, 'that is the finest music in the world.'

JAMES STEPHENS, *Irish Fairy Stories*

Contents

Note on Titles

The Irish poems in manuscript do not have titles. Most translators use titles suggested either by the subject or by the context of the original. Where a translation is untitled, the first line of the poem in Irish is provided in square brackets.

Introduction

Around 850 CE in a monastery in Switzerland, an Irish scribe – whose name we don't know – scribbled some verses on the bottom margins of Priscian's *Latin Grammar*:

> *Domfarcai fidbaide fál fomchain lóid luin nad cél*
> *huas mo lebrán indlínech fomchain trírech innanén . . .*

> *Fommchain cói menn medair mass himbrot glass*
>   *de dindgnaib doss*
> *debrath nomchoimmdiu cóima caínscríbaimm forroída r[oss]*

He may be composing a poem there and then. If so, we can see from the manuscript (*see* Notes and Sources) that he's made a revision by inserting *fidbaide* and thereby altered the metre. It's an intriguing possibility that we are witnessing the composition of a poem in Irish nearly 1,200 years ago. But of course it's equally likely he's writing the poem, whether his own or someone else's, from memory, and is correcting an omission. It's also possible that it is just a fragment, a quotation, not a poem at all.

The 'poem' then, let's say. It was first printed and commented on in 1853 by the German philologist Kaspar Zeuss, and it was turned into English by Whitley Stokes and John Strachan in 1903. Even from their functional (and slightly inaccurate) translation, one recognises its quality:

> A hedge of trees surrounds me: a blackbird's lay sings to me
>   – praise which I will not hide –
> above my booklet the lined one trilling of the birds sings to me.

> In a gray mantle the cuckoo's beautiful chant sings to me from
>   the tops of bushes:
> may the Lord protect me from Doom! I write well under the
>   greenwood.

It presents an idyll of creativity and contentment in harmony with
the natural world. The sentiment would translate to almost any
period of English poetry, perhaps most readily to the mid-
seventeenth century. It has been translated several times in our
own time, and the version by Ciaran Carson (2 in this anthology)
shows its lyrical stamina:

> all around me greenwood trees
> I hear blackbird verse on high
> quavering lines on vellum leaves
> birdsong pours down from the sky
>
> over and above the wood
> the blue cuckoo chants to me
> dear Lord thank you for your word
> I write well beneath the trees

Now it is a poem, surely. As such, it is in keeping with what we
have of poetry in Old Irish.

From around the late seventh century a new type of poem was
being written in Irish monasteries. It is distinct from what is
known of the traditional poetry composed by the professional
poets, the *filid*. They used accentual rhythm. These new 'monastic'
poets counted syllables; they wrote in stanzas, usually four lines;
and they used rhyme. Lyricism and a feeling for nature are
characteristic of this 'monastic' poetry, economy and strictness of
form typical of its style. Poetry as practised by the monks is a
literary art, metrically sophisticated and consciously patterned

with intricate alliteration and assonance. It was written by book men, and also bookwomen, who lived in religious communities. They were learned poets and knew they had a readership of like-minded people.

No doubt these poets were familiar with the traditional poetry. One of the earliest datable poets, Colmán Mac Lénini, who died around 600, was a *file* who also founded the monastery of Cloyne. It seems likely that many subsequent monastic poets also came from 'bardic' families and may have trained in the secular schools. We can assume the secular poetry was meant for performance and often had an encomiastic purpose. It may also have had a ritualistic function, as has been suggested by James Carney, in invoking the seasons; it probably served other similar druidic purposes; and it was certainly regarded, and feared, as a satirical weapon. But the monastic poetry was without a public function. Its concern is with the viewpoint of the individual. A few of the poems are religious but many aren't, though they are typically written in a Christian context and are compatible with faith. Some explore the tension between religious and secular outlooks. The majority address a range of familiar themes: love, desire, aging, grief, exile.

Here we have something new in the post-classical world, a founding moment in western European poetry: poems for contemplative reading, written for the eye as well as the ear; poems, too, that look inward to the reflective consciousness, while also, remarkably, rejoicing in the enjoyment of the senses. They can express a flash of perception, or a moment of coarse humour; but they also have resort to argument, suggestion, irony, that is to say sophisticated literary devices, making their appearance in vernacular poetry for the first time.

The lyricism of a number of these poems, together with their feeling for nature, has led to speculation and counter-speculation. For Kenneth Hurlstone Jackson, 'Manchan's Wish' (15) is sincere expression of feeling, the work of a hermit living in the wilderness who is following an ascetic lifestyle; whereas for Donnchadh Ó Corráin its author is a busy monastic prelate, being playful and ironic as he entertains the fantasy of a retreat from the world. The truth is we know almost nothing about these poets' lives. And it is all too easy to fill the enigmatic silence occupying the margins of their poems with our imaginings. Frank O'Connor and David Greene, for instance, suggest that the author of 'Myself and Pangur' (3) was Sedulius Scottus, since he was on the Continent around the time of its composition. They further surmise that on his journey from Ireland he may have stopped off in Wales, where he acquired the white cat – Pangur, they explain, is Welsh for 'fuller'. It is the immediacy of these poems, their vivid impression of 'felt life', that no doubt tempts one to give them such fictionalised scenarios.

I can't resist adding two of my own speculations about Old Irish poetry. One is that the concentration and perfection of the lyrics depend on the value given to each word. This is due, at least in part, to the visual sense of a written word as a discrete entity. The Irish scribes were the first to put spaces between words (it made learning Latin easier); and this practice, this physical shift in awareness, transforms how one writes, and reads, a poem. Just think of the effect it would have if we were now to return to the lengthy chains of letters known in antiquity. The single word-unit is easily moved, or substituted; it becomes more practicable, with intent and skill, to make elaborate metrical patterns and to construct the tight-knit stanza. These poets loved metres, as is evident from the metrical tracts they produced; and they specialised in stanzaic form, especially the quatrain – which would become almost the exclusive stanza of Irish verse until the eighteenth century (and indeed it remains a favoured vehicle of lyric poetry).

My other conjecture has to do with the benign depiction of nature we find in early Irish poems. This isn't invariably the case: bad weather is also a subject, as is the power of the sea, and the threat of a Norse raid. But the general picture is of a sunny paradisal island, where one can live in the woods on nuts, berries, and watercress. One reason for this was that the weather was good, relatively. The golden age of the monasteries coincided with the gradual warming that led to the Medieval Warm Period from around 950 to 1250, when much of the extant literature was produced. It was that same warming of the North Atlantic, of course, that facilitated the Vikings, whose raids brought intermittent terror throughout the ninth and tenth centuries. The monasteries were equally vulnerable to attack from native chieftains, whose rivalries and power struggles maintained a state of chronic low-level warfare. Ireland was hardly a peaceable kingdom. Even so, a sense of the island as a *locus amoenus* took hold and a space opened up for an exquisite lyrical flowering that was, and remains, a unique contribution to the European imagination. Here are poems with a primary delight in the raiment of the seasons, in light itself, the songs of birds, the company of one's fellow creatures. No doubt there were complex sources for this Edenic awareness. But I'd tentatively suggest it helped that you could live outdoors without hunger or fear or dependency, and you could travel about on foot without hardship.

You could also take to the sea in the summer months. The Irish invented a specific genre of sea-narrative, the *immram*. These are a type of wonder tale involving contact with the otherworld, with its gods and its timeless dimension. One of the earliest is the eighth-century *Immram Brain* (The Voyage of Bran), whose verse is represented here (49). It may be that some folk memory of the *Odyssey* informs these narratives. But they are *sui generis*, compositions of unprecedented fantastical invention, as exemplified in the enchanted fortress of 'The Island of the Glass Bridge' (50) and the eerie islands in Tennyson's versification of 'The Voyage of Maeldune' (51).

The most famous of the *immrama* is in Latin, the *Navagatio sancti Brendani abbatis*, written around 900, which reputedly inspired Columbus – as it certainly inspired Tim Severin to build a medieval-style boat in 1976 and follow St Brendan's route around the North Atlantic to sail, successfully, to America.

Travellers the Irish monks undoubtedly were, if not to America, then to Iona and the north-east of England, to the Carolingian court, deep into the Continent to join or found monastic communities: St Colm Cille, St Columbanus, Sedulius Scottus, John Scottus Eriugena. It is worth clarifying in passing that epithet '*Scottus*'. North-eastern Ireland and western Scotland once formed the kingdom of Dál Riata. It was founded in the fifth century, and flourished in the sixth and into the seventh. Throughout medieval times, Ireland, Gaelic-speaking Scotland, and the Isle of Man had a common culture (a shared heritage reflected in this anthology by several Scottish translators). From around 900 the entire region had a common language. Our present-day sense of separate nationality is a late-medieval development. The vigorous Christian culture of this north-western region was exported to Europe as a revitalising and civilising influence for centuries, and with it came the new poetry, with its metrical invention and lyrical appeal.

Only a handful of Old Irish poems are known (here 1, 2, 3, 7, 39, and 42) from these contemporaneous continental sources. But they offer one area of solid ground in an otherwise fluctuating world of textual uncertainty. Were the anonymous monks who penned them skiving from the real work at hand, the drudgery of copying and glossing? Kuno Meyer quotes a colleague, W. M. Lindsay, on the subject of the Irish 'marginalia':

[T]hese entries are written in the top margins of the pages as clearly and carefully as the text itself. And that is a curious thing. How came the head of the scriptorium to allow his monks to spoil a manuscript by so prominent insertions of trivialities? It almost makes one guess that he must have been ignorant of Irish, i.e. that the MS. was written in a continental monastery where the authorities were continental, and that the Irish strangers felt they could play pranks with impunity. When asked what he had written the scribe would point to the Latin pious sentences on the preceding top margins and say 'merely the Irish equivalents of sentences like these'.

What scamps they were! But perhaps they were engaged in an intriguing form of transmission, a sort of early Dropbox system, whereby poems were placed where they could be accessed by the next passing *Scottus*, and so had a tiny discerning readership? We don't know. Even so, it must have been thrilling for a young man from Iona or Bangor arriving at Laon or Carinthia, after months of hazardous travel, to come upon verses in his own language, a poem he might know from school, or perhaps one he'd never seen.

And then no one came. No more 'Irishmen', no more *Scotti*. '*Domfarcai fidbaide fál*' and its like were there unread, not understood, not recognised as verse, for about 900 years until German philologists in the nineteenth century took an interest in their language.

*

Of the remaining poems in the anthology over half come from Old Irish, the period 600 to 900, and are 'contemporary' with those iconic poems of continental provenance. The rest are Middle Irish (900–1200) and later. All of these poems survive in insular manuscripts. They present a complicated story of transmission, since none of the manuscripts are from before 1100. The three oldest sources date from the early twelfth century: *Lebor na hUidre* (The Book of the Dun Cow); The Book of Leinster; and Rawlinson B 502. By then the monasteries were in decline and their libraries and treasures were about to be dispersed or destroyed. *Lebor na hUidre* was compiled at Clonmacnoise around 1100. Its head scribe is recorded as killed there in 1106.

The most common sources for Old Irish poems date from the fifteenth, sixteenth, and early seventeenth centuries. So, with respect to the earliest poems, we are dealing with manuscript transmission extending some six or seven hundred years, in uncertain circumstances, through political upheavals and steady linguistic change. Even so, Gerard Murphy has pointed out that a sixteenth-century scribe can be as reliable a source for a ninth-century text as a twelfth-century one.

Undoubtedly, the transmission of the ancient texts was bolstered by veneration for books and a conservative attitude to the past. Among the oldest manuscripts from Ireland is a psalter from the sixth century, traditionally said to have been written by Colm Cille – an unlikely though not impossible ascription, as he died in 597. It is known as *An Cathach*, The Battler, a name it acquired because it was carried into battle by the O'Donnells of Donegal, a talismanic practice that continued for perhaps 1,000 years. Although the psalter contains no poems in Irish, it does testify to the value placed on old books, as well as the precarious circumstances in which they were damaged or, often, destroyed.

Irish manuscripts would have led risky, nomadic lives after the disappearance of the monasteries in an island without universities, cities, or indeed fortresses to protect them. They were copied and re-copied, with perhaps a tendency to update, clarify, reinvent, competing with the underlying preservative instinct. Inevitably, those texts that made it did so in a degraded condition, encrusted with later verbal and grammatical forms, and with many so-called *cruces desperationis* marking those *loci deperditi*, places where a true reading is irretrievable.

When we turn to the Middle Irish poems, the picture is somewhat less frustrating. Not surprisingly, more poems survive than from the earlier centuries. In some cases, we find near-contemporaneous texts, such as 'Loeg's Description of Mag Mell' (48), a late-eleventh-century poem whose text Gerard Murphy prints from *Lebor na hUidre* more or less 'as it stands in the manuscript'. But such instances are rare. More typical are the texts of the *Acallam na Senórach* (The Conversation of the Elders), the most extensive extant work in Middle Irish, which exists in variant manuscripts from the fifteenth century and later.

The Middle Irish period of these poems is one that has acquired its own literary characteristics, as well as having features in common with the past. The lyrical spirit of the monastic poetry continues in typically vivid observation of nature, expressions of religious feeling, as well as recollections of pagan lore. There was a widespread cult of Colm Cille in the eleventh and twelfth centuries, and numerous lyrics, of variable merit, are attributed to him. The later poetry, generally, is inconsistent in quality, with a tendency to prolixity and elaboration superseding the exemplary economy and restraint of poems in Old Irish. It is of course one of the effects of translation to erase not only the linguistic differences between the earlier and later poems but also to disguise the stylistic differences. In translation there is little to separate the eighth-century verses of the Voyage of Bran from those of the Voyage of Maeldune 200 years later; or to distinguish the lovely 'blackbird' poems of different centuries.

One twelfth-century work, however, stands out as something quite novel: *Buile Suibne* (The Madness of Sweeney). This is also an example of conservative tradition. Sweeney was a king of the seventh century, who reputedly went mad at the Battle of Mag Rath in 639. He had quarrelled with St Ronan, who cursed him, and as a result he changed to a bird and lived in the wilderness. A stock of legends and poems grew up around him. One such poem indeed is 'The Oratory' (1), from the ninth century, preserved in the same Austrian source as 'Myself and Pangur'. *Buile Suibne* itself is a prose-and-verse tale from around 1175 and it has many of the features of a medieval romance. Neither the prose nor the verse is of consistent quality. But the underlying mythic appeal of the story is robust: Sweeney's fate of being cursed by a cleric has resonated with many modern Irish poets, and his life of extremity in the wilderness, alone but close to nature, is remarkable for its combination of hardship and exhilaration. It has attracted several notable translators, among them Robert Graves and Seamus Heaney; and the exploits and verses of the feathered madman are woven into the comic invention of Flann O'Brien's *At Swim-Two-Birds*.

Another twelfth-century romance of exceptional originality is *Aisling Meic Conglinne* (The Vision of Mac Conglinne), which is also a prose-and-verse narrative. This is a somewhat crude work whose inconsistencies are offset by the appeal of its core idea. It draws on motifs from *immram* and the 'wonder tale', but does so for parodic and humorous purposes. As such, it has connections with contemporary Goliardic poems, sharing their spirit of entertainment, hearty excess and gleeful irreverence. It may itself have been a seminal work of medieval literature. Its mock-voyage to a 'land of plenty' (52) surely influenced the fourteenth-century Norman-Irish poem *The Land of Cockayne*, and thereby much subsequent literature.

*

A legend concerning the *Táin Bó Cúailnge*, the great Old (and Middle) Irish prose-and-verse saga, relates how it was lost and only recovered through the miraculous agency of St Colm Cille and St Ciaran of Clonmacnoise. Senchán Torpéist, Chief Poet of

Ireland (in 598 as it happens), was obliged under the terms of a curse to recite the *Táin* but could find no one who knew it in its entirety. He called on the saints for help. Colm Cille summoned one of the protagonists, Fergus Mac Róich, from his grave. Fergus duly recited the *Táin*. Meanwhile Ciaran slaughtered and skinned his pet cow, and he wrote the tale down on the hide. And so we have The Book of the Dun Cow. Thus was the lost masterpiece reclaimed as a unitary and incontestably authoritative text.

A legend, alas. The Book of the Dun Cow does indeed contain a version of the *Táin*, but it is incomplete and not the work of a single author. The legend encapsulates the Sisyphean job of recovering the ancient literature. Something great and wonderful has been lost. There is an obligation that it be recovered. But its restoration demands, in the end, something beyond the ordinary – a miraculous intervention.

The task of recovering early Irish poems in the form in which they were written has been ongoing since those first German philologists, whose heroic endeavour of scholarship culminated in the supreme achievements of Kuno Meyer (1858–1919). Gerard Murphy's *Early Irish Lyrics* (1956) and James Carney's *Medieval Irish Lyrics* (1967), supplemented by his other publications, are more recent landmarks in providing authoritative texts, and in a form accessible to the non-specialist. David Greene and Frank O'Connor's *A Treasury of Irish Verse* (1967) takes a somewhat maverick approach, but it has also been influential in establishing the canon as it currently stands.

'Canon', however, is a misleading term in this context. In many instances, the editors are interventionist and speculative, even 'creative' when arriving at a coherent reading of a poem. Gerard Murphy was at times openly intrusive in producing conjectural results, as in his editing of 'The Nun of Beare' ('Song of the Woman of Beare', 25). His stated principle was to arrive at a date for a poem's composition, and then to 'construct a text which at least would not shock the original author'. It is an approach that has not gone uncontested. As James Carney puts it, 'a licence to emend . . . may in practice become a licence to create'.

One notable example of Murphy's practice is his edition of 'May-Day', translated here by T. W. Rolleston as 'The Song of Finn in Praise of May' (58), which he 'reconstructed in accordance with ninth century standards' from its fifteenth-century manuscript. Carney's subsequent edition of this poem undoes the process and in fact accords very closely with the manuscript. But he also interprets it as an accentual poem, and dates it as 'hardly later than the early seventh century' and 'possibly belong[ing] to the sixth', making it a very early poem indeed. Ironically, Rolleston's resourceful translation attempts 'to render the riming and metrical effect of the original', but the original it renders is that of Meyer's edition of 1904, and what it approximates, accordingly, is the syllabic metre *debide* common in later poems. In effect, this poem proves an elusive target for the translator: it has moved back and forth, been 'translated' in the root sense, within Irish.

Carney himself, despite his rebuke to Murphy, is lured readily enough into creative editing. This can produce a brilliant result, as in his reading of 'The Priest Rediscovers His Psalm-Book' (19), a poem ostensibly addressed to a lover, which he interprets, persuasively, as an elegant literary conceit. In other instances, his practice is more questionable. For example, the brief text of 'India' (46) has been extracted arbitrarily from a lengthy topographical poem. Greene and O'Connor are the most intrepid in their ambitious remaking of texts. With respect to 'The Nun of Beare', they formed the view that the poem had been mutilated by 'a dotty eleventh century editor' and 'attempted a complete textual re-arrangement', an undertaking which, perhaps fortunately, they abandoned.

What we see, then, is that poems can be in flux within Irish. It seems the search for a single authoritative text is often chimerical. It is also, arguably, misguided in that the concept of an 'original' is not useful in the context of much early Irish literature. The transmission of texts over centuries occurred within a culture that revered the past, certainly, but without any means, or need, for those linear markers we now employ to maintain a sense of 'objective' history. It was a culture where the distinction between a historical figure and his legendary afterlife was happily blurred. For instance, as we have seen, it was common for twelfth-century transcribers, or authors, to put 'Colm Cille cecinit' above a poem; or to ascribe it to Suibne, or indeed Finn. No doubt the practice was meant to give the text pseudo-authority. But it also befits a mentality that permits a lively interaction between present and past, one where a historical person might pop up centuries after his death, or indeed centuries before it. The fabric of reality is porous. Wondrous feats of travel and time-travel are the norm. It's a world-view more congenial to sci-fi than it is to classical scholarship.

An editor's pursuit of the 'original' resists a natural fluidity within the tradition, when it might make more sense to let a text roam freely in time. To cite one example of editorial herdsmanship, 'Grainne's Lullaby' survives in a single seventeenth-century source, the beautiful *Duanaire Finn* (Songbook of Finn), compiled at Leuven in 1627. It is in modern Irish. This is the poem that was printed and translated by Eoin MacNeill in 1908. His text and translation are the basis for Eleanor Hull's 'The Sleep-Song of Grainne Over Dermuid' (64), a rather florid if still eloquent version (though the reader would be advised to overlook the sentimental ending).

Frank O'Connor tells us Yeats's 'Lullaby' is an adaptation of the same poem. Yeats uses the opening line to launch into his own personal and classicising mythology. It is a very free 'take' on the poem indeed; too free, it seemed, for inclusion. Even so, if we want the truest approximation to the bewitching music of the Irish, we find it here:

> Sleep, beloved, such a sleep
> As did that wild Tristram know
> When, the potion's work being done,
> Roe could run or doe could leap
> Under oak and beechen bough,
> Roe could leap or doe could run [. . .]

Gerard Murphy restored the text of the poem in *Duanaire Finn* to its twelfth-century 'original'. That there is a Middle Irish text underlying the modern one is something we can take on trust from Murphy. But that 'original' may itself have a source in the tenth century, when we know a version of a saga devoted to the love triangle involving Finn, Grainne and Diarmuid existed. So what we have is a chain of 'originals', one of which is the text in modern Irish, and the chain might be said to extend to Hull's version and Yeats's poem.

*

'Grainne's Lullaby' belongs to the Fenian cycle, to *fiannaigheacht*, the vast stock of poetry and lore associated with the exploits of Finn mac Cumhaill and his retinue. This is an aspect of Irish tradition that is best characterised by its fluidity. Stories relating to Finn and his followers were known in the Old Irish period, though only tantalising fragments survive. It may be that there existed then, or earlier, a unitary body of written material that was lost.

But Fenian lore survived by other means. The tradition continued to be reinvented in written form over the centuries, notably in the *Acallam na Senórach* (The Conversation of the

Elders), which brings the Fenian cast into contact with St Patrick and Christianity. It dates from around 1200. One of the richest later sources of *fiannaigheacht* is *Duanaire Finn* mentioned above. This was compiled at an interesting – and fateful – moment in the history of Irish culture. It was commissioned by Somhairle Mac Domhnaill and compiled by Aodh Ó Dochartaigh. These men were 'wild geese', expatriates soldiering in Europe's wars after the collapse of the Irish kingdoms at the start of the seventeenth century. It can be seen as an act of cultural retrieval at a moment of political defeat.

Apart from these core repositories, Fenian lore became widely dispersed throughout Gaelic Scotland and Ireland. There are many manuscript sources. But there was also, of course, a popular and ubiquitous oral tradition. The 'lays of Fionn' were part of folk music or were sung to the accompaniment of the harp in aristocratic houses. Fenian lore continued to be an important part of the repertoire of the *seanchaí*, or traditional storyteller, up to the present day.

We can assume there was interaction, a good deal of to and fro over the centuries, between oral transmission and written texts. After 1750, however, the practice of Anglophone collecting of oral material introduces a new dynamic. It necessarily requires translation. And this quickly manifests itself as literary translation, with attempts to reproduce the imaginative effect of the source material. One could think of Macpherson's *Ossian* in this context, not as straightforward forgery but as a legitimate instance of *fiannaigheacht*, where the lore passes from oral to written form and is reinvented in the transition. Standish O'Grady's recasting of Fenian stories as prose romances a century later is scarcely different, though it is transparent. It could be argued that Yeats in his early years was working along similar lines to Macpherson. He took his material from both the folklore he collected and from books, mainly Eugene O'Curry's lectures on the *Manuscript*

Materials of Ancient Irish History (1861). Both folk and scholarly material are sources for the poems devoted to Fenian subjects in *The Wanderings of Oisin* and *The Wind Among the Reeds*.

*

But now we have crossed the divide: Irish poetry in English. A language has been 'lost', a culture, its literature. The great counter-effort of recovery, with its implication of 'recuperation', is under way. Something of the glory of the old literature must be restored, albeit in the language that has displaced it. 'Translation' here has not just a literary function (though it has that); it is also an act of patriotic responsibility with political implications and imperatives. It is less concerned with fairly reflecting the literature of the past in its otherness and integrity – not to mention the gaps and uncertainties – than with adumbrating a proud heritage, with the aim of projecting a unitary national destiny that encompasses both languages.

The decades of the Revival, between 1880 and 1930, are replete with versions and adaptations from Irish of all periods. It's been argued that the inventiveness of its great writers was energised by the psychological need to create a distinct literature freed from the colonial parent. They were engaged in an act of sustained cultural parricide. In terms of translations, the same motivation and energy prompted several late-Victorian attempts at stylistic novelty that now seem, too often, merely late-Victorian. What we have are mostly linguistic oddities, such as the prose romances of Standish O'Grady, Standish Hayes O'Grady's *Silva Gadelica*, and Lady Gregory's self-styled 'Kiltartanese' in her versions from Irish. The verse translations of the period generally suffer from similarly misguided distortions, but dotted here and there are occasional gems, such as Alfred Perceval Graves's 'The Song of Crede' (28) and Thomas MacDonagh's 'Eve' (26), poems that read naturally and exemplify the principle of attentive translation without resort to excessive stylistic exertion.

Although the ideological pressures of the Revival eased, there remains something exquisitely paradoxical about the translation of Irish into English. The creative effort of finding the adequate 'equivalent' harbours the intimate knowledge of betrayal; it carries in it the desire that the new language should not be 'English' somehow. The paradox is represented in Brian Friel's *Translations*, where the Irish characters on stage speak in English but maintain the dramatic illusion that they are speaking Irish (and cannot understand their fellow actors). As a translator one yearns to create the same illusion, so that the actual treachery in words should be trumped by fidelity on some extra-linguistic plane. To pull off that stunt, one would surely need the intervention of Colm Cille and Ciaran.

Instead, the poet-translator wrestles mundanely with requirements of form and idiom in what one must accept, perhaps grudgingly, is the mother tongue, while also attempting to reach across to the manifest qualities of these ancient poems. There's no crime in creating wonderful poems with a loose link to Irish originals, as Yeats and others have done. But the translator wants to do more. One must hope to open a window into the imaginative moment of the Irish poem, while also wishing for a slice of luck so that the new version stands in English.

In making this selection, I have looked for translations – both time-honoured and new – that manage some such miracle. I've chosen those that read as poems in English, in the first place. But I have certainly favoured versions that respect the source. One wants to find the prose sense of the Irish at least present in the translation. I have also looked for an awareness of the shape and sound of the Irish poem. Yet the extent to which a translator seeks to replicate metre and rhythm is bound to vary. One notable translation not in my selection is Seamus Heaney's 'The Blackbird of Belfast Lough':

The small bird
Chirp-chirruped:
Yellow neb,
   A note spurt.
Blackbird over
Lagan water,
Clumps of yellow
   Whin-burst!

The Irish survives as an example of an intricate metre, *snám súad* (swimming of sages), which Heaney imitates with ingenuity. I have preferred a version by Derek Mahon (10), though in part because it's the only translation of Old Irish I'm aware of by this poet. It's a version that nods towards Irish versification but does so in the form of a single regular quatrain.

Poets use what they know when translating, and rightly draw on their own voices and tonalities. The extent to which the translator brings a personal idiom to bear on the translation is a variable and potentially contentious aspect of the process. The range here is illustrated by the inventive slant of Paul Muldoon's 'Myself and Pangur' in contrast to the straight approach of Eiléan Ní Chuilleanáin's 'Song of the Woman of Beare'. One specifically vexed aspect of translating the early texts is the use of titles. These are a conventional imposition in modern editions and in translations. The poems in manuscript are untitled, though many are embedded in prose, and so they come with a narrative context that readily suggests a title, such as 'Cáel's Praise of the House of Créide' (67). Others survive with a scribal note that may suggest the title; this is the case, for example, with 'Manchan's Wish' (15). Elsewhere, given a choice, I have preferred titles that are 'factual' and editorially neutral such as 'Bell' or 'Storm', or else translations have been left untitled. In the latter case, the first line from the original Irish is used in square brackets.

All the translators had to work (so far as I can tell) without the helping hand of Colm Cille. The result is not a unitary representation of the early poetry but a book in many voices. It is, one hopes, a fitting embodiment for our own time of the vitality of this poetry, among the oldest and most enduring cultural achievements on these islands. It is also, of course, provisional: translations inevitably decay with the conventions of their day, and the act of translation is in any case infinitely repeatable in principle. These versions of the early lyrics enter the continuum of Irish tradition, adding their contribution to an unfinished patchwork that is destined to expand and change in future generations.

M.R.

THE FINEST MUSIC

1

The Oratory

I wouldn't swap my tree-haunt
in Tuam Inver for a mansion.
I've the stars to give me light,
the sun or moon as companion.

My cell's the work of craftsmen
known for providing shelter –
the dearest Lord of Heaven
is its architect and thatcher.

I've no fear of a downpour,
and no dread of battle spears
here under the ivy bower
where I've found a home outdoors.

*c.*800   MAURICE RIORDAN

2

The Scribe in the Woods

all around me greenwood trees
I hear blackbird verse on high
quavering lines on vellum leaves
birdsong pours down from the sky

over and above the wood
the blue cuckoo chants to me
dear Lord thank you for your word
I write well beneath the trees

9th c.   CIARAN CARSON

3

Myself and Pangur

Myself and Pangur, my white cat,
have much the same calling, in that
much as Pangur goes after mice
I go hunting for the precise

word. He and I are much the same
in that I'm gladly 'lost to fame'
when on the *Georgics,* say, I'm bent
while he seems perfectly content

with his lot. Life in the cloister
can't possibly lose its lustre
so long as there's some crucial point
with which we might by leaps and bounds

yet grapple, into which yet sink
our teeth. The bold Pangur will think
through mouse-snagging much as I muse
on something naggingly abstruse,

then fix his clear, unflinching eye
on our lime-white cell wall, while I
focus, in so far as I can,
on the limits of what a man

may know. Something of his rapture
at his most recent mouse-capture
I share when I, too, get to grips
with what has given me the slip.

And so we while away our whiles,
never cramping each other's styles
but practising the noble arts
that so lift and lighten our hearts,

Pangur going in for the kill
with all his customary skill
while I, sharp-witted, swift and sure,
shed light on what had seemed obscure.

c.800   PAUL MULDOON

4

Bee

A tremor of yellow from blossom to blossom
   the day-shift bee stays out with the sun
then booms across the darkening valley
   to his happy date with the honeycomb

8th–9th c.   PATRICK CROTTY

5

Summer

Summer's come strong in limb
green weighs down branch and stem
up jump the spotted deer
blue seals swim the clear sea

The cuckoo calls all day
the nights bring sound rest
and swallows skim the hedge
when herds go out to graze

Leave the sheiling's stove
stags are on the move
on the long white strand
white combers roll to land

Listen to the winds blow
high in Drumdell's oaks
while mares down in Kilcove
are trotting with new foals

Green foams from brown bark
leafing are the purple shoots
now summer's here, winter past
holly snags the stag's hoof

The blackbird guards a brood
in her bothy in the wood
a calm overtakes the sea
and salmon course upstream

Now sunshine clothes the crags
the seedling splits the hull
hounds bay, stags in packs
ravens fat, summer's come

9th–10th c.   MAURICE RIORDAN

6

Autumn

Fall is no man's travelling time;
Tasks are heavy; husbandmen
Need horses as the light grows less;
Lightly their young drop from the deer,
    Dandled in the faded fern;
Fiercely the stag stalks from the hill,
Hearing the herd in clamorous call.
Cobbled the mast in windless woods;
Weary the corn upon its canes,
    Colouring the brown earth.
Endless the thorns that foul the fence
That frames the hollow of some house;
The heavy ground is filled with fruit,
And by the fort, hard from their height,
    Hazelnuts break and fall.

11th c.   FRANK O'CONNOR

7

[Is aicher in-gáeth in-nocht]

Wind fierce to-night.
Mane of the sea whipped white.
I am not afraid. No ravening Norse
On course through quiet waters.

9th c.   SEAMUS HEANEY
                & TIM O'NEILL

8

[Fégaid úaib]

Look far, cast
Eyes northeast
Over tossed
    Seascapes.

There's the seal.
And tides fill
And run, all
    Whitecaps.

9th c.   SEAMUS HEANEY

9

Storm

Storms lash Manannan's strong back
now the winds have left their caves
and roam the broad sea plain
spears in hand ready to start
        cold winter's campaign.

The aspect of Lir's kingdom
troubles our small garrison.
The storm's onset frightens them
for nothing but the great doom
        can outstrip such ruin.

When the wind is from the east
the sea-god becomes possessed.
Waves speed to the far world's edge,
the fiery ridge in the west
        where the sun finds rest.

When the wind is from the north
the ice-mountains break their bonds
chasing the current southward
to gain warm skies where the songs
        of seabirds are heard.

When the wind is from the west
it crosses the black abyss
and races past us to grasp
from sea-empires of the east
       the sun-tree's fortress.

When the wind is from the south
it soars above the Saxons,
the warriors of iron shields,
to smite Skid and bind a shroud
       round bleak Mount Brandon.

High seas, the tide at full force,
stately ships at anchor groan
now the sand-laden gale whips
waves to foam near Inver's coast
       where the stout helm snaps.

Men wake fearful of omens.
They dread the tempest's toll
when the tide is swan-plumed
above the sea-monsters' home
       and Fand's hair is loosed.

The flood's fury is unleashed,
every river mouth is wrecked,
as the destroying hand strikes
Scotland, Cantyre's rocky head,
       with white-capped peaks.

Son of the Father, king of hosts
shield me from eternal harm.
Lord of the Communion feast
save me from the icy blast,
        from Hell's bitter storm.

11th c. or earlier   MAURICE RIORDAN

10

The Bangor Blackbird

Just audible over the waves
a blackbird among leaves
whistling to the bleak
lough from its whin beak.

9th c.   DEREK MAHON

11

[Int én gaires asin tsail]

Birdsong from a willow tree.
Whet-note music, clear, airy;
Inky treble, yellow bill –
Blackbird, practising his scale.

9th c.   SEAMUS HEANEY

12

[Ach a luin is buide duit]

Lucky blackbird with your nest
hidden in the green forest
a monk who rattles no bell
clear, happy is your whistle

11th–12th c.   MAURICE RIORDAN

13

Calendar of the Birds

Birds of the world –
any hour when January's young
a throng trills from the gloomy wood
welcoming the sun.

On the splendid 8th of April
pure swallows meet us again,
rekindling the controversy:
since October 8th, what's hidden them?

On Ruadan's feast, good to say,
their bonds are loosed;
on 17th May the first cuckoo calls
from the tangled wood.

In Tallaht, birds pause their songs
on the nones of July; a day of woe
when the living pray to Mael Ruain
spared by the Badb-crow.

On Ciaran's day – carpenter's son –
the brent goose crosses the chilly sea;
on the feast of wise St Cyprian
the dun stag bells from the red heath.

Six thousand years
the world has seen;
the oceans will overwhelm everywhere
at end of night, as birds keen.

Musical the melody they make
praising God the King,
the shining Lord of high heaven.
Listen: wide and far the bird-choirs sing.

8th–9th c.   KATHLEEN JAMIE

14

The Praises of God

How foolish the man
Who does not raise
His voice and praise
With joyful words,
As he alone can,
Heaven's High King.
To Whom the light birds
With no soul but air,
All day, everywhere
Laudation sing.

11th c.   W. H. AUDEN

15

Manchan's Wish

Oh Son of the living god,
ever-abiding king
I long for a hut in the wildwood
to dwell therein.

A bothy, and beside it,
for the washing away of sin
by grace of the holy spirit:
a clear flowing burn with a linn.

The beautiful greenwood
cloistering every side,
where many-voiced songbirds
might flit and hide.

Facing the warm south,
with stream-fed lands
bountiful and beneficent
for every plant.

A few sterling youths
– let me number them –
humble and obedient
to worship the King,

to meet every need:
four threes, three fours;
two sixes in the church:
one south, one north,

six pairs besides myself,
ever offering praise
to the King, who commands
the sun's rays.

A lovely church, linen-draped;
home for heaven's God
with a lamp lit bright
above the pure white Book.

One house to visit
to attend the body's needs,
with no impure thoughts
or shameful deeds.

The husbandry I'd freely
undertake and choose: leeks
fresh and fragrant, hens,
speckled salmon, bees –

Sufficient food and raiment
from the fair-famed King;
– to remain there a while,
praying to Him.

10th c.   KATHLEEN JAMIE

[23]

16

[M'óenurán im aireclán]

Solitary in a small cell,
perfectly alone –
I'd love such a pilgrimage
before death calls.

A concealed distant hut
where I'd crave to be forgiven;
untroubled conscience
facing holy heaven.

With body purified,
manfully tramped down,
eyes weak with weeping
in amends for my desires,

with all passions shriveled,
the wanton world denied,
and eager, ardent mind
I would petition god.

To heaven in the clouds
I'd send sincerest laments,
confessions devout and earnest,
tears in fierce bouts.

A bed fearful and cold
like a doomed man's,
short fitful slumber,
frequent, early prayer.

As to property and food –
lovely abstinence;
nothing occasioning sin
need pass my lips.

9th c.   KATHLEEN JAMIE

17

Bell

Little bell
clinking through the gusty night:
sweeter your call
than a wanton girl's moan of delight.

9th c.   PATRICK CROTTY

18

Unruly Thoughts

Shame on my thoughts,
        constantly at play!
I dread what their wild sports
        will bring me on Judgement Day.

During psalms, they stravage
        down every wrong road;
they roister, they rampage
        in full sight of God.

At assemblies, at parties
        of frivolous women,
through woodlands, through cities,
        they go storming.

Along pleasant avenues
        lightly they saunter;
down paths not in common use,
        I tell you, they blunder.

Without a boat, they will hop
        across the wide ocean;
in one bound, fly up
        from earth to heaven.

Fearing nothing,
        they foolishly roam,
then from their profligate outings
        hurry back home.

Though you try to constrain them
　　　　or shackle their feet,
they lack the discipline
　　　　to keep still and be quiet.

Neither blade nor flail
　　　　will cow them: sinuous
as an eel's tail
　　　　slipping through my fingers.

Neither lock nor dungeon
　　　　nor iron chain,
neither moat nor bastion
　　　　will make them refrain.

Dear Christ, in your chastity
　　　　and all-seeing wisdom,
may your sevenfold ministry
　　　　help me resist them.

Take command of my heart,
　　　　God who made all,
till I love you as I ought
　　　　and do your will.

Admit me, Christ,
　　　　to your blessed company,
you who are true and worthy of trust –
　　　　unlike me.

10th c.   CHRISTOPHER REID

19

MAEL ÍSU Ó'BROLCÁN, d. 1086

The Priest Rediscovers His Psalm-Book

How good to hear your voice again,
   Old love, no longer young, but true,
As when in Ulster I grew up
   And we were bedmates, I and you.

When first they put us twain to bed,
   My love who speaks the tongue of Heaven,
I was a boy with no bad thoughts,
   A modest youth, and barely seven.

We wandered Ireland over then,
   Our souls and bodies free of blame,
My foolish face aglow with love,
   An idiot without fear of blame.

Yours was the counsel that I sought
   Wherever we went wandering;
Better I found your subtle thought
   Than idle converse with some king.

You slept with four men after that,
   Yet never sinned in leaving me,
And now a virgin you return –
   I say but what all men can see.

For safe within my arms again,
    Weary of wandering many ways,
The face I love is shadowed now
    Though lust attends not its last days.

Faultless my old love seeks me out;
    I welcome her with joyous heart –
My dear, you would not have me lost,
    With you I'll learn that holy art.

Since all the world your praises sings,
    And all acclaim your wanderings past
I have but to heed your counsel sweet
    To find myself with God at last.

You are a token and a sign
    To men of what all men must heed;
Each day your lovers learn anew
    God's praise is all the skill they need.

So may He grant me by your grace
    A quiet end, an easy mind,
And light my pathway with His face
    When the dead flesh is left behind.

10th c.   FRANK O'CONNOR

from Marbhan and Guaire

KING GUAIRE
My brother Marban, hermit monk,
why don't you sleep in a bed
instead of among pine-trees, with only the forest floor
on which to lay your tonsured head?

MARBAN THE HERMIT
As it happens, I have a hut in the forest.
Its precise location
is known only to God, but I can report
that on one side an ash-tree stands guard
while the other is barred
by a hazel such as you'd find at a ring-fort.

Heather stands in for its doorposts
and fragrant honeysuckle
binds its lintel fast.
For the benefit of the pigs
beech-trees let fall beech-twigs
and pig-fattening mast.

The dimensions of my hut –
small but not *too* small –
make it easy enough to defend.
A woman in the guise of a blackbird
spreads the word
from its gable-end.

The great stags of Drum Rolach
start up from a stream that runs
across a mud-shelf.
From there you may make out
clay-red Roigne, Mucruime and, no doubt,
the plain of Moenmag itself.

Won't you come for a tour
of my wooded realm
with its paths only wild beasts beat?
Though I know
you have much more to show,
my life is quite replete.

Think of the shaggy limbs
of a yew-tree
saying its sooth.
Think of a massive oak
spreading a green cloak
by way of a summer-booth.

You may ponder a huge apple-tree such
as you'd find at another ring-fort.
A tree bestowing many gifts.
When it comes to nuts,
the hazel-trees by my hut
never give short shrift.

There are the best of wells
and lovely waterfalls
over which to gush.
The medicinal yew
and hackberry on which to chew
are nowhere more lush.

In the vicinity are goats,
stags and hinds,
pigs that are the next best thing to pets
and wild pigs lurking in the scrub,
the badger-sow and her cubs
in their sett.

In front of my establishment
a great host of the countryside peaceably assembles.
They gather. They gather and fold.
Meanwhile the dog-fox
picking its way through the wood in long socks
is lovely to behold.

In the face of the quickly prepared repasts
on offer in my house
I couldn't be more devout.
The water's superb,
as are the perennial herbs
that accompany salmon and trout.

The rowan or mountain ash.
The blackthorn and the sloes
within its scope.
Acorns in an acorn heap.
A bunch of bare berry-sheep
dangling from bare mountain slopes.

A handful of eggs,
honey, more beech-mast, heath-pease
God's sent my way.
There are even more apples to prog,
cranberries from the bog,
and berries known as whortle-, bil-, or blae-.

Beer flavoured with bog myrtle.
A bed of strawberries the only bed
from which joy is evinced.
Hawthorn good for a pain in the heart.
Yew for giving it a start.
Blackthorn tea for a medicinal rinse.

How lovely then to quaff a cup
of hazel-mead
from the very freshest batch.
To nibble at more acorns
and blackberries among the flailing thorns
of the bramble patch.

In next to no time summer has come round
with its dense groundcover
and all it bespeaks.
The tastes of wild marjoram
and, near the pond-dam,
blood-cleansing wild leeks.

Bright-breasted woodpigeons
will be billing and cooing
in a lovely rush.
Over my abode
the default mode
of a mistle-thrush.

Bees and beetles,
their low level hum
as if through a screen.
Brent geese and barnacle geese
disturbing the peace
just before Halloween.

A lithe little linnet
working his magic
from the hazel branch.
It's on an open door the flock
of variegated woodpeckers knock.
They give themselves carte blanche.

Now white seabirds come flying,
herons and gulls
and the sea-airs they bruit.
Far from down in the dumps
is the grouse's thump
through red heather-shoots.

Then the heifer lowing
in high summer,
daylight on the gain.
Life is far from tough
when we've more than enough
from the bounteous plain.

The call of the wind
through a wood's wickerwork.
Clouds that somehow prevail.
A river that falls
through rocky walls
on such a pleasant scale.

Beautiful, too, the pine-trees
that give me music
without my making a pitch.
However wealthy you may be
Christ has left me
no less rich.

Though you delight
in having more treasures
than might easily have sufficed,
I'm quite content
with what is lent
me by that self-same Christ.

I have none of the aggravation
or din of battle
by which your heart-strings are constantly cut,
only gratitude to the Lord
for the gifts he affords
me in my hut.

KING GUAIRE
I will give my kingdom
and all that's due
to me from Colman for the rest of my days
to live, Marban, as you.

9th c.   PAUL MULDOON

21

Jesus and the Sparrows

The little lad, five years of age
– Son of the living God –
Blessed twelve puddles he'd just then coaxed
From water and from mud.

Twelve statuettes he made next;
'Sparrows shall you be named'
He whispered to those perfect shapes
That Sabbath in his game.

'Who plays with toys this holy day?'
A Jew scowled at the scene
And marched the culprit straight to Joseph
To scold his foster-son.

'What sort of brat have you brought up
That wastes his sacred time
Scrabbling in mud on the Sabbath Day
To make bird-dolls from slime?'

At that the lad clapped two small hands
And with sweet piping words
Called on the dolls before their eyes
To rise as living birds.

No music ever heard was sweeter
Than the music from his mouth
When he told those birds 'Fly to your homes
To east and west and south'.

The story spread throughout the land
And is heard down to this day
And all who hear it still can hear
The sparrows' voices pray.

8th c.   PATRICK CROTTY

22

St Ite's Song

Jesukin
stays with me day out, day in;
no loutish priest-spawned lodger he
but my own dear Jesukin.

I did not get this wounded heart
from fostering just anyone;
Jesu and high heaven's gang
curl up with me when day is done.

Jesu gives me every good
and he gets a just return;
you try praying to any other
and in eternity you'll burn.

No Partholán, Aedh or corner boy
is nurtured in my secret shade
but Jesu, bright angel-headed
son of the Judaean maid.

Sons of puffed-up priests and chiefs
plead for my sweet fostering
but why would I waste time on them
when all my care is Jesukin?

Sweet-singing girl choirs, lift
your most melodious hymn
to Jesu lord of heaven's height
asleep here in my bosom.

*c.*900   PATRICK CROTTY

23

The Downfall of Heathendom

Ailill the king is vanished
    Vanished Croghan's fort,
Kings to Clonmacnois
    Come to pay their court.

In quiet Clonmacnois
    About Saint Kieran's feet
Everlasting quires
    Raise a concert sweet.

Allen and its lords
    Both are overthrown,
Brigid's house is full,
    Far her fame has flown.

Navan town is shattered,
    Ruins everywhere;
Glendalough remains,
    Half a world is there.

Ferns is a blazing torch,
    Ferns is great and good,
But Beg, son of Owen,
    And his proud hosts are dead.

Old haunts of the heathen
  Filled from ancient days
Are but deserts now
  Where no pilgrim prays.

Little places taken
  First by twos and threes
Are like Rome reborn,
  Peopled sanctuaries.

Heathendom has gone down
  Though it was everywhere;
God the Father's kingdom
  Fills heaven and earth and air.

Sing the kings defeated!
  Sing the Donals down!
Clonmacnois triumphant,
  Cronan with the crown.

All the hills of evil,
  Level now they lie;
All the quiet valleys
  Tossed up to the sky.

*c.*800 *Félire Oengusso*   FRANK O'CONNOR

[42]

24

The End of Clonmacnois

'Whence are you, learning's son?'
'From Clonmacnois I come
My course of studies done,
    I'm off to Swords again.'
'How are things keeping there?'
'Oh, things are shaping fair –
Foxes round churchyards bare
    Gnawing the guts of men.'

11th c.   FRANK O'CONNOR

25

Song of the Woman of Beare

Low tide. As with the sea.
Age darkening my skin.
Even as I struggle
Age grabs and likes its meal.

I am the nun of Beare.
The shirt I wore was fresh
Always. Today I'm worn,
An old shirt sees me out.

The main chance, the money
Draws your love not the man;
In our day flourishing
Our joy was the human.

Human goodness pleased us,
Delight on our journeys
Wearing out days with them
And no boasting after.

Look at them now: they crow,
They claim, they do not yield,
They part with little, then
Boast of how much they gave.

Carriages, prizewinning
Fast racehorses, the gifts
Of those high days: God bless
The giver's open hand.

And now my body craves
Homing to where it's known;
Let the Son of God choose
The time to claim me back.

These bony slender arms
Of mine – the ones I once
Owned, how they used to like
Embracing those great kings.

As they look now, my arms
Are slender and bony,
Hardly worth the trouble
Lifting to hug young boys.

Girls are glad to welcome
May as it draws near;
This season saddens me,
Pitiful, an old one.

I don't join in sweet chat;
No bride-feast is prepared;
Thinning and grey my hair
Suits the cheap veil on it.

I don't object: a white
Veil covering my head
Rather than colours I
Wore in my drinking days.

The old attract no envy –
But what about Feimen;
I wear out old clothing,
Feimen is clothed in flowers.

The Stone of Kings in Feimen,
Rónán's hall in Bregon:
Long the storms are beating
Weathered ancient faces.

The wave on the high sea
Roaring, raised by winter,
Forbids all visits now:
High and low keep away.

I know what they're doing,
Rowing over and back;
The reeds of Áth Alma,
They sleep in a cold place.

The sea I sailed on, those
Days, was youth – long ago.
Years took my looks from me,
Cooled my first young ardour.

The time is long today,
Even when the sun shines
I need my covering,
I am feeling my age.

Summer of youth I knew,
I wore out, then autumn,
Winter that ages all,
I feel it beginning.

I wore out my youth first,
And glad I did. How would
My dress be newer now
If I had played safer?

It was a fine green dress
My king spread on Drumain;
The worker knew his craft,
Coarse stuff turned to new wool.

And I am in sadness
– Each acorn must decay –
I feasted with candles
But the chapel is dark.

My days drinking spirits
And wine with kings are gone.
Now it's a soft drink, whey,
Water with the seniors.

I'll stick with the soft drinks,
God's will limiting me,
Living God let me pray,
Keep me far from anger.

My dress is marked by age,
My sense is gone astray,
My hair is grey, I'm like
An old tree's withered bark.

My right eye was taken
To buy eternal land
And now the left eye goes
To complete the payment.

The wave at high tide, then
The tide falling again –
What high tide fills for you
Is emptied by low tide.

The wave at high tide, then
Falling tide that follows:
I know them, I have seen
Full tide and low water.

The wave at high tide – how
Silent my store-house now:
Once I fed multitudes,
A hand fell on them all.

The Virgin's son – who knew
He would enter my house?
If I did no good deed,
No one had refusal.

Man among the creatures
Is most to be pitied,
Never foresees low tide
When the tide is fullest.

I have had my high tide,
I have held to my trust,
Jesus Mary's son has
Saved me from low-tide grief.

Well for islands at sea,
Their high tide follows low
Water; I do not hope
My tide will turn and flow.

Hardly a harbour now
Seems familiar to me;
All that the high tide saw
Low water drags away.

*c.*800   EILÉAN NÍ CHUILLEANÁIN

26

Eve

I am Eve, great Adam's wife,
I that wrought my children's loss,
I that wronged Jesus of life,
Mine by right had been the cross.

I a kingly house forsook,
Ill my choice and my disgrace,
Ill the counsel that I took
Withering me and all my race.

I that brought winter in
And the windy glistening sky,
I that brought sorrow and sin,
Hell and pain and terror, I.

11th c.   THOMAS MacDONAGH

27

Líadan Laments Cuirithir

Joyless
what I have done;
to torment my darling one.

But for fear
of the Lord of Heaven
he would lie with me here.

Not vain,
it seemed, our choice,
to seek Paradise through pain.

I am Líadan,
I loved Cuirithir
as truly as they say.

The short time
I passed with him
how sweet his company!

The forest trees
sighed music for us;
and the flaring blue of seas.

What folly
to turn him against me
whom I had treated most gently!

No whim
or scruple of mine
should have come between

Us, for above
all others, without shame
I declare him my heart's love.

A roaring flame
has consumed my heart:
I will not live without him.

9th c.   JOHN MONTAGUE

28

The Song of Crede

These are the arrows that murder sleep
At every hour in the night's black deep;
Pangs of Love through the long day ache,
All for the dead Dinertach's sake.

Great love of a hero from Roiny's plain
Has pierced me through with immortal pain,
Blasted my beauty and left me to blanch
A riven bloom on a restless branch.

Never was song like Dinertach's speech
But holy strains that to Heaven's gate reach;
A front of flame without boast or pride,
Yet a firm, fond mate for a fair maid's side.

A growing girl – I was timid of tongue,
And never trysted with gallants young,
But since I have won into passionate age,
Fierce love-longings my heart engage.

I have every bounty that life could hold,
With Guare, arch-monarch of Aidne cold,
But, fallen away from my haughty folk,
In Irluachair's field my heart lies broke.

There is chanting in glorious Aidne's meadow,
Under St Colman's Church shadow;
A hero flame sinks into the tomb –
Dinertach, alas my love and my doom!

Chaste Christ! that now at my life's last breath
I should tryst with Sorrow and mate with Death!
At every hour of the night's black deep,
These are the arrows that murder sleep.

*c.*800   ALFRED PERCEVAL GRAVES

29

[Cride hé]

He is my love,
   my sweet nutgrove:
a boy he is –
   for him a kiss.

9th–10th c.   MICHAEL HARTNETT

30

Deirdre's Lament for the Sons of Usnach

The lions of the hill are gone,
And I am left alone – alone –
Dig the grave both wide and deep,
For I am sick, and fain would sleep!

The falcons of the wood are flown,
And I am left alone – alone –
Dig the grave both deep and wide,
And let us slumber side by side.

The dragons of the rock are sleeping,
Sleep that wakes not for our weeping:
Dig the grave and make it ready;
Lay me on my true Love's body.

Lay their spears and bucklers bright
By the warriors' sides aright;
Many a day the Three before me
On their linkèd bucklers bore me.

Lay upon the low grave floor,
'Neath each head, the blue claymore;
Many a time the noble Three
Redden'd those blue blades for me.

Lay the collars, as is meet,
Of their greyhounds at their feet;
Many a time for me have they
Brought the tall red deer to bay.

Oh! to hear my true Love singing,
Sweet as sound of trumpets ringing:
Like the sway of ocean swelling
Roll'd his deep voice round our dwelling.

Oh! to hear the echoes pealing
Round our green and fairy sheeling,
When the Three, with soaring chorus,
Pass'd the silent skylark o'er us.

Echo now, sleep, morn and even –
Lark alone enchant the heaven! –
Ardan's lips are scant of breath, –
Neesa's tongue is cold in death.

Stag, exult on glen and mountain –
Salmon, leap from loch to fountain –
Heron, in the free air warm ye –
Usnach's Sons no more will harm ye!

Erin's stay no more you are,
Rulers of the ridge of war;
Never more 'twill be your fate
To keep the beam of battle straight.

Woe is me! by fraud and wrong –
Traitors false and tyrants strong –
Fell Clan Usnach, bought and sold,
For Barach's feast and Conor's gold!

Woe to Eman, roof and wall! –
Woe to Red Branch, hearth and hall! –
Tenfold woe and black dishonour
To the false and foul Clan Conor!

Dig the grave both wide and deep,
Sick I am, and fain would sleep!
Dig the grave and make it ready,
Lay me on my true Love's body.

8th–9th c.   SAMUEL FERGUSON

COLM CILLE

31

BECCÁN THE HERMIT, d. 677

Last Verses in Praise of Colum Cille

He brings northward to meet the Lord a bright crowd of chancels –
Colum Cille, kirks for hundreds, widespread candle.

Wonderful news: a realm with God after the race,
a grand kingdom, since He's set out my life's progress.

He broke passions, brought to ruin secure prisons;
Colum Cille overcame them with bright actions.

Connacht's candle, Britain's candle, splendid ruler;
in scores of curraghs with an army of wretches he crossed
    the long-haired sea.

He crossed the wave-strewn wild region, foam-flecked,
    seal-filled,
savage, bounding, seething, white-tipped, pleasing, doleful.

Wisdom's champion all round Ireland, he was exalted;
excellent name: Europe is nursed, Britain's sated.

Stout post, milk of meditation, with broad actions,
Colum Cille, perfect customs, fairer than trappings.

On the loud sea he cried to the King who rules thousands,
who rules the plain above cleared fields, kings and countries.

In the Trinity's care he sought a ship – good his leaving –
on high with God, who always watched him, morning, evening.

Shepherd of monks, judge of clerics, finer than things,
than kingly gates, than sounds of plagues, than battalions.

Colum Cille, candle brightening legal theory;
the race he ran pierced the midnight of Erc's region.

The skies' kind one, he tends the clouds of harsh heaven;
my soul's shelter, my poetry's fort, Conal's descendant.

Fame with virtues, a good life, his: barque of treasure,
sea of knowledge, Conal's offspring, people's counsellor.

Leafy oak-tree, soul's protection, rock of safety,
the sun of monks, mighty ruler, Colum Cille.

Beloved of God, he lived against a stringent rock,
a rough struggle, the place one could find Colum's bed.

He crucified his body, left behind sleek sides;
he chose learning, embraced stone slabs, gave up bedding.

He gave up beds, abandoned sleep, finest actions;
conquered angers, was ecstatic, sleeping little.

He possessed books, renounced fully claims of kinship:
for love of learning he gave up wars, gave up strongholds.

He left chariots, he loved ships, foe to falsehood;
sun-like exile, sailing, he left fame's steel bindings.

Colum Cille, Colum who was, Colum who will be,
constant Colum, not he a protector to be lamented.

Colum, we sing, until death's tryst, after, before,
by poetry's rules, which gives welcome to him we serve.

I pray a great prayer to Eithne's son – better than treasure –
my soul to his right hand, to heaven, before the world's people.

He worked for God, kingly prayer, within church ramparts,
with angels' will, Conal's household's child, in vestments.

Triumphant plea: adoring God, nightly, daily,
with hands outstretched, with splendid alms, with right actions.

Fine his body, Colum Cille, heaven's cleric –
a widowed crowd – well-spoken just one, tongue triumphant.

7th c.   THOMAS OWEN CLANCY

32

[Fil súil nglais]

Towards Ireland a grey eye
Will look back but not see
Ever again
The men of Ireland or her women.

11th c.   SEAMUS HEANEY

33

[Is aire charaim Doire]

Derry I cherish ever.
It is calm, it is clear.
Crowds of white angels on their rounds
At every corner.

12th c.   SEAMUS HEANEY

34

Colm Cille in Scotland

A blessing to lie on the breast of an island
     at its naked tip
and see there below the shimmering
     face of the deep;

to see wide-swelling waves
     of weighty water
raise a hymn in their ancient style
     to heaven's Father;

to see the level yellow sands
     where land meets sea
and hear miraculous birdsong
     call me;

to hear the endless thunder
     of waves breaking
and the hollow cry round the churchyard
     of winds shrieking;

to see the glorious flocks take wing
     above the ocean
and out of nowhere a whaleschool
     in marvellous motion;

to see the vast flux of tide that ebbs
     and floods untiring
and know that it was I 'who turned
     his back on Ireland';

to writhe in remorse at merest
thought of home
and count my secret failings,
all of them;

to bless our precious Lord and God
in sole command
of heaven's ranks of choiring angels,
earth's sea and land;

to bend in study for virtue's sake
over my psalter
then lend a while to chanting psalms,
a while to prayer,

a while to thinking of heaven's Prince
our living Saviour,
a while to bustling out of doors
at light labour,

a while to stripping dulse from rocks,
a while to fishing,
a while to work among the poor,
a while to confessing

until God sets up within my breast
His real presence
and the King I'll always serve makes
each thing blessèd.

early 12th c.   PATRICK CROTTY

35

Colmcille on Exile

It would be such a blast, O Son of God,
to be able to scud
across the heavy seas
to Ireland, to go back to the exquisite

Plain of Eolarg, back to Benevanagh,
to go back across the Foyle
and listen to the swans
singing at full

tilt as my boat, the Dew-Red,
puts in to port,
with the very seagulls coming out
for a ticker tape parade.

I sigh constantly to be in Ireland,
where I still had some authority,
rather than living among foreigners,
dejected, dog-tired.

A pity, O King of Mysteries,
I was ever forced off my home turf,
a pity I ever got caught up
in the Battle of Cul Dreimhne.

Isn't it well for Cormac of Durrow
to be back there in his cell
and listening to the self-same sounds
that once lifted up my soul,

the wind in the elm-tree
getting us into the swing,
the blackbird's droll lamentation
as it claps its wings,

the early morning belling
of a herd of big bucks,
the music of summer edging through woodland
from the cuckoos' beaks . . .

The three things I left behind
I liked best on earth
were Durrow, Derry of the heavenly choirs,
and Gartan, my place of birth.

I so loved being in Ireland
and still rail against being displaced.
To hang with Comgall in Bangor, Canice in Kilkenny,
it would be such a blast.

11th c.   PAUL MULDOON

36

The Scribe

My wrist is stiff from writing,
from keeping the nib's path true
as the pen's thin beak squirts
its jet of beetle-bright juice.

A spring of wisdom spurts from
my brown hand in fair copy,
when I sprinkle on vellum
ink of the green-skinned holly.

I send my leaky pen to work
on good books without skiving.
I serve men of greater worth,
my wrist's stiff from writing.

12th c.   MAURICE RIORDAN

37

Mo Ling's Way

When I find myself with the elders
I lay down the law against fun;
when I wind up with the clubbers
I go-go like the youngest one.

10th c.   PATRICK CROTTY

38

Advice to Lovers

The way to get on with a girl
   Is to drift like a man in a mist,
Happy enough to be caught,
   Happy to be dismissed.

Glad to be out of her way,
   Glad to rejoin her in bed,
Equally grieved or gay
   To learn that she's living or dead.

FRANK O'CONNOR

39

[Isém linn indiu]

Such a lovely day
I pause to let the sun's rays
illumine my page

9th c.   MAURICE RIORDAN

40

[Ro-cúala]

It's a no-brainer
he won't give horses for retainer
he'll pay as his likes do now
a cow

9th c.   MAURICE RIORDAN

41

[Atá ben as-tír]

There's a lady in these parts
whose name I'm slow to divulge
but she's known to let off farts
like stones from a catapult

?10th c.   MAURICE RIORDAN

42

[Téicht do róim]

You go to Rome
but the reward is scant.
You find the King you want
was one you left back home.

9th c.   MAURICE RIORDAN

43

The King of Connacht

'Have you seen Hugh,
The Connacht king in the field?'
'All that we saw
Was his shadow under his shield.'

FRANK O'CONNOR

44

The Drowning of Conaing

The great cleansing waves of the sea
have swept over the land.
They've ganged up on Conaing
in his frail ash-frame currach.

She who smothered with her white mane
Conaing in his fragile currach
has set her wry smile
against the sacred ash of Tortu.

early 8th c. *Annals of Ulster 621 CE*   PAUL MULDOON

45

Cú Chuimne

Cú Chuimne in youth
Read his way through half the Truth.
He let the other half lie
While he gave women a try.

Well for him in old age.
He became a holy sage.
He gave women the laugh.
He read the other half.

Annals of Ulster 746 CE   JOHN V. KELLEHER

46

AIRBERTACH MAC COISSE, d. 1021

India

Its bounty of diamonds and lodestones
known throughout the world,
its pearls strung from shore to shore . . .
Ore beds. Its precious garnets.

The unicorn's stuck in a rut
but the breeze is mild beside
the wide swaths its ferocious elephants carve.
Harvest-time comes twice a year.

late 10th c.   PAUL MULDOON

47

The Wooing of Etain

Fair lady, will you travel
To the marvellous land of stars?
Pale as snow the body there,
Under a primrose crown of hair.

No one speaks of property
In that glittering community:
White teeth shining, eyebrows black,
The foxglove hue on every cheek.

The landscape bright and speckled
As a wild bird's eggs –
However fair Ireland's Plain,
It is sad after the Great Plain!

Warm, sweet streams water the earth,
And after the choicest of wine and mead,
Those fine and flawless people
Without sin, without guilt, couple.

We can see everyone
Without being seen ourselves:
It is the cloud of Adam's transgression
Conceals us from mortal reckoning.

O woman if you join my strong clan,
Your head will hold a golden crown.
Fresh killed pork, new milk and beer,
We shall share, O Lady Fair!

late 9th c. JOHN MONTAGUE

48

Loeg's Description of Mag Mell

on my great journey I came
        to a fortress passing fair
a peopled hill whereon I found
        Labraidh of the flowing hair

there he sat upon the hill
        his throng of weapons close at hand
beyond compare his yellow hair
        fastened by a golden band

he knew me when he saw my face
        from a purple fivefold cloak
will you go with me said he
        to the royal house of oak

two kings dwell there Failbe Finn
        and Labraidh whom you know of old
each with a great entourage
        two peoples in one fold

to the right are fifty beds
        fifty couches at their feet
to the left are fifty beds
        fifty couches at their feet

a border of blood-red beds
        white posts crowned with gold
a candle stands before each one
        a glowing precious stone

horses standing to the west
        the portal where the sun goes down
one troop grey with speckled manes
        another of a chestnut brown

at the east door three trees stand
        with foliage of purple glass
from which perpetual birds sing out
        to all the royal youths that pass

at the gateway to the fortress
        is a most praiseworthy tree
illuminated by the sun
        in branches of gold filigree

there are sixty trees all found
        topmost branches intertwined
from which abundant mast falls down
        to feed three hundred healthy swine

in that fort there is a store
        of three times fifty speckled cloaks
and at the throat of every cloak
        gleams a brooch of speckled gold

there is a vat of merry mead
        being given out among the clan
never ending is that source
        ever full for every man

the daughter of the house
        is beautiful beyond compare
has many skills and graces
        and free-flowing yellow hair

her conversation is so
        wonderful everyone falls
in love with her no wonder
        everyone is in her thrall

then said she whose is this boy
        we do not know this charioteer
are you Cú Chulainn's boy perhaps
        if so you may draw near

slowly I approached for fear
        I'd prove unworthy of her grace
the son of Dechtire she said
        will he be coming to this place

sad for him he did not go
        that time they sought him high and low
for then he also would have seen
        the noble homestead I have seen

were all of Ireland mine
        could I but dwell from whence I came
what matter all of Ireland then
        I'd give it all away

late 11th c.   CIARAN CARSON

49

Manannán
from The Voyage of Bran

Manannán sang these verses to Bran:

Bran thinks it marvellous to sail
        his coracle over a clear sea
while for me my swift chariot
        drives over a flowery plain

Bran cleaves the clear sea
        with the prow of his keen boat
while for me the Plain of Delights
        heaves with a thousand flowers

over a clear sea Bran beholds
        wave after rolling wave
while on the Plain of Feats I see
        a host of crimson-headed flowers

while the seahorses' white manes
        are combed by Bran's roving eye
flowers pour forth streams of honey
        in Manannán Mac Lir's domain

the glassy sea where you are found
　　　　the shining ocean that you sail
is blossoming with green and yellow
　　　　truly it is solid ground

those speckled salmon leaping
　　　　from the womb of the white sea
truly they are calves and lambs
　　　　sporting without enmity

though you see but one charioteer
　　　　on the many-flowered plain
you do not see the many steeds
　　　　abroad on its broad bosom

a huge army shimmers on the plain
　　　　brimming with every colour
banners of silver and cloths of gold
　　　　in jubilant array

shaded by the spreading trees
　　　　men and women freely play
a game of such delight and ease
　　　　they know no sin nor wrong

along the top of a waving wood
　　　　has your coracle sailed
under the keel of your little boat
　　　　are trees laden with fruit

a wood of blossom and bud
　　　　bearing the scent of the true vine
an imperishable wood
　　　　glorious with leaves of gold

since the human race began
　　　　this ageless keep has been
we do not expect its imminent decease
　　　　untainted as we are by sin

woe the day the serpent came
　　　　to the first man in his residence
twisting the bright world to the fall
　　　　of that dark consequence

greed and lust his overthrow
　　　　a noble offspring ruined
the wasted body goes to the fold
　　　　of everlasting pain

in a world of overweening pride
　　　　the living believe in the living
forgetting God the havoc of disease
　　　　and spiritual death by cunning

deliverance shall come from Him
　　　　who made the music of the spheres
he shall be man and God he shall breathe
　　　　His word upon the seas

the form you see me in now
        shall come to your domain
a journey lies in store for me
        to meet the woman of the plain

a human figure sways in the chariot
        Manannán Mac Lir who says
that from his seed shall spring a man
        embodied in bright clay

Manannán shall lie with Cáintergen
        in agile congress and be summoned
to his son in the bright world and Fíachna
        shall take him as his son

he shall be known in every fairy fort
        regaled in all the territories
coursing in wisdom he shall report
        deep mysteries fearlessly

he shall come in the shape of every beast
        both on blue sea and on land
a dragon before the enemy
        the wolf of every great forest

he shall be a silver-antlered stag
        on a field of driving chariots
a speckled salmon in a deep pool
        a sleek seal and a snow-white swan

through the centuries to come
       he shall be king he shall lay low
the battlements beyond the tomb
       his great wheels shall plough

a red swathe through the battlefield
       among kings and warriors
he shall be proclaimed hero
       Manannán his mentor

he whose time in this body shall be
       but fifty years in this world
who is laid low by a dragonstone
       in the battle at the stronghold

shall crave a drink from Loch Ló
       he shall suffer a gush of blood
he shall be swept by the angelic host
       up through the clouds to the feast

therefore let Bran row steadily on
       it is not far to the Land of Women
and before sunset he shall reach Emain
       and its manifold pleasures

8th c.   CIARAN CARSON

50

The Island of the Glass Bridge

they rowed to an island
        guarded by a stronghold
girded by a bronze fence
        that was something to behold

around the fence a shining moat
        stood high above the sea's white mane
while over it a glass bridge soared
        oh what a splendid tale

brimming with self-confidence
        the younger men dashed up its span
thus suffering the consequence
        of sliding back the more they ran

then lightsome and lissom
        a white-throated woman
came gliding to meet them
        with swanlike elegance

the hem of her fair cloak
        shimmered like golden wheat
and sandals of silver
        ornamented her feet

upon her breast she wore a brooch
       of wondrous white silver
inlaid with woven gold
       of intricate workmanship

her head of yellow hair
       gleamed like the finest gold
so graceful her footsteps
       it seemed her body flowed

at this end of the great bridge
       as in a holy place
under an imposing lid
       was a well clear as glass

she poured cupfuls of liquor
       as one would for a feast
but offered none to drink
       which was puzzling to say the least

Germán of the great voice
       spoke fitting words to her
we're a little surprised
       as to why we're not served here

whereupon she vanished
       and closed her noble fort
while from her silver net
       sweet music issued forth

the choir under her sway
       lullabied them to sleep
she appeared the next day
       unblushingly woman

thus they lay as they were
        for three days and three nights
and still her music played
        with no mead-hall in sight

she brought them to a mansion
        above the raging sea
to where they were regaled with wine
        and a marvellous meal

with graceful demeanour
        she spoke powerful names
giving each man the honour
        of his personal name

when they clamoured for her
        to slake their leader's lust
she said sin was a thing
        she viewed with disgust

unholy as you are
        unorthodox your creed
ask the secret of the island
        that I might tell and you might heed

they woke in the rowboat
        after morning had come
wondering not knowing
        where the island had gone

*c.*920   CIARAN CARSON

from The Voyage of Maeldune

(founded on an Irish legend, 700 CE)

III

And we came to the Silent Isle that we never had touch'd at
  before,
Where a silent ocean always broke on a silent shore,
And the brooks glitter'd on in the light without sound, and the
  long waterfalls
Pour'd in a thunderless plunge to the base of the mountain walls,
And the poplar and cypress unshaken by storm flourish'd up
  beyond sight,
And the pine shot aloft from the crag to an unbelievable height,
And high in the heaven above it there flicker'd a songless lark,
And the cock couldn't crow, and the bull couldn't low, and the
  dog couldn't bark.
And round it we went, and thro' it, but never a murmur, a breath –
It was all of it fair as life, it was all of it quiet as death,
And we hated the beautiful Isle, for whenever we strove to speak
Our voices were thinner and fainter than any flittermouse-shriek;
And the men that were mighty of tongue and could raise such
  a battle-cry
That a hundred who heard it would rush on a thousand lances
  and die –
O they to be dumb'd by the charm! – so fluster'd with anger
  were they
They almost fell on each other; but after we sail'd away.

IV

And we came to the Isle of Shouting, we landed, a score of
    wild birds
Cried from the topmost summit with human voices and words;
Once in an hour they cried, and whenever their voices peal'd
The steer fell down at the plow and the harvest died from
    the field,
And the men dropt dead in the valleys and half of the cattle
    went lame,
And the roof sank in on the hearth, and the dwelling broke
    into flame;
And the shouting of these wild birds ran into the hearts of
    my crew,
Till they shouted along with the shouting and seized one
    another and slew;
But I drew them the one from the other; I saw that we could
    not stay,
And we left the dead to the birds and we sail'd with our
    wounded away.

*c.*920   ALFRED LORD TENNYSON

52

from The Vision of Mac Conglinne

It is a meaningful vision I had last night. If you give me a break I'll go on. Manchin, the king's right hand man, said 'No way', but the incorrigible poet continued with what the angel made manifest to him anyway:

> What a mind-blowing, mouth-watering trip,
> what a feast for the eyes, what a vision
> I had, let me tell you.
> A boat of solid suet
> was moored in a creamy cove
> above the world's calm ocean.
>
> We boarded that cog, charged out
> to sea on the choppy surface,
> pulling hard on the oars
> across the milky plains,
> leaving a wake of seaweed,
> a spume of honey-colored sand.
>
> We reached a fabulous fort
> with ramparts of thick custard
> on the other side of the water.
> A drawbridge made of fresh butter,
> the embankment of harvest wheat,
> the palisades of juicy rashers.

The whole structure was spot on,
rising mighty there.
I entered under
the stringy drapes of dry meat,
over a threshold of croutons.
Its wall was made of cottage cheese.

Its pillars of moldy blue
were set in boiled crubeens
– trotters trotting one after the other.
Joists of thick curd,
rafters of frozen yogurt
supported the whole show.

There was a well of wine at the back
and a stream of mead and mulled ale.
No tastier watering hole.
There were hops for brewing stout.
On top of all that was a spring of malt
brimming from the floor.

A pool of colcannon
under a thick batter
lay between that and the ocean.
It was bordered by wedges of butter
glazed with lard
on the outer wall.

Rows of aromatic apple trees,
a rosy orchard in full bloom,
flourished between it and the hill.
A garden of veggies – leeks,
cabbages, carrots, and onions –
grew at the back as well.

[95]

It was a warm, bright household
full of foxy, well-fed men
lounging around the hearth.
Seven torcs and collars
of cheese, tripe and drisheen
adorned each man's neck.

The lord of the manor,
dressed in a corned-beef cloak,
stood next to his elegant wife.
The head chef was there also
at the sizzling spit,
a huge fork strapped to his back.

The good king would appreciate
a bard reciting at the dinner table,
an enjoyable performance,
a real treat
to hear that lay of the boat
voyaging Milky Sea.

Manchin wised up as it dawned on him that the reciting of such a
corker vision would coax the demon of gluttony from the king's
swollen belly and save their world . . .

*c.*1100   GREG DELANTY

SWEENEY THE WILD MAN

53

from Verses Attributed to Suibne Geilt

A rich tuft of ivy
   climbs through a twisted tree.
If I were at the very top
   I would be frightened to come out.

I fly before the larks,
   running hard and lively.
I leap across the reeds
   up on the mountain tops.

The proud wood-pigeon
   when it rises up before me
I overtake it suddenly
   now that my feathers have grown.

When the stupid clumsy woodcock
   rises up before me,
I see a raging enemy
   in the blackbird raising alarm.

And every time I leap
   down onto the ground
I see the little fox
   down there chewing bones.

Fiercest of dogs, he would catch me
   quickly in the ivy
except I leap so swiftly
   up to the mountain peak.

Little foxes creeping
   up toward me and away,
and wolves moving about
   – I fly from the very sound!

They tried to overtake me
   coming running hard,
but I fled away before them
   along the mountain peaks.

My sin comes against me
   everywhere I turn
and I learn, as I weep,
   I'm a sheep without a fold.

12th c.   THOMAS KINSELLA

54

Suibne and Éorann

SUIBNE

At ease you are, bright Éorann,
Bound bedward to your lover;
It is not so with Suibne here –
Long has he wandered footloose.

Lightly once, great Éorann,
You whispered words that pleased me.
'I could not live,' you said, 'were I
Parted one day from Suibne.'

Now it is clear and daylight clear,
How small your care for Suibne;
You lie warm on a good down bed,
He starves for cold till sunrise.

ÉORANN

Welcome, my guileless madman,
Dearest of humankind!
Though soft I lie, my body wastes
Since the day of your downfall.

SUIBNE

More welcome than I, that prince
Who escorts you to the banquet.
He is your chosen gallant;
Your old love you neglect.

ÉORANN

Though a prince may now escort me
To the carefree banquet-hall,
I had liefer sleep in a tree's cramped bole
With you, Suibne, my husband.

Could I choose from all the warriors
Of Ireland and of Scotland,
I had liefer live, blameless, with you
On watercress and water.

SUIBNE

No path for his beloved
Is Suibne's track of care;
Cold he lies at Ard Abhla,
His lodgings cold are many.

Far better to feel affection
For the prince whose bride you are,
Than for this madman all uncouth,
Famished and stark-naked.

ÉORANN

I grieve for you, toiling madman,
So filthy and downcast;
I grieve that your skin is weather worn.
Torn by spines and brambles . . .

O that we were together,
And my body feathered too;
In light and darkness would I wander
With you, for evermore!

12th c.   ROBERT GRAVES

55

Suibne in the Trees

When I hear the belling
    of the stag in the glen
my heart begins
    to pine and keen.

Acorns taste
    as sweet as ever
and I still savour
    the hazel's coffer,

but unmet lust
    and unseasoned grief
mar a man's life
    when his home is lost.

Silver birch, waltz
    in the wind that scatters
aspen leaves
    like staves in a battle.

Apple tree, apt
    to be looted by boys,
weather the storm
    with the rowan blossom.

Alder, shield me
    with your pallid branches.
Blackthorn, bless me
    with blood-dark sloes.

Ivy, hold yourself
   close as a halter.
Yew, stand to,
   at odds with the world.

Holly, be a shelter
   from the wind, a barrier.
Ash, be a spear-shaft
   hurled by a warrior.

Dearly it cost me
   to cross you, briar:
a scald of blood money,
   my palm in bloom.

Hateful to me
   as an evil word:
a rootless tree
   holding sway in the wood.

12th c.   PAUL BATCHELOR

56

The Man of the Wood

SWEENEY
What happened, Man of the Wood,
to make you whinge
and hobble like this? Why did
your mind unhinge?

MAN
Caution and fear of the king
have silenced me.
I made a tombstone of my tongue
to keep my story.

I am the Man of the Wood.
I was famous
in battles once. Now I hide
among bushes.

SWEENEY
I come from the Bush myself.
I am Sweeney,
son of Colman. Like yourself,
outcast, shifty.

12th c.   SEAMUS HEANEY

57

The Rough

I love the merry roar of the Rough
when it's fighting against the tide,
when fish-shoals come with the flood
and thrash about the rocky bed.

It's a sight to fire my blood up
when the ocean's incoming rush
meets the torrent of the Rough,
and knocks it back with a shove.

They butt and bite like champions
going at it hammer and tongs,
flood and cold ebb all night long.
But neither gets the upper hand.

I hang on for the deep freeze.
Then it's showtime on the river
when I sleep close to the noise
of revellers in starlit weather –

to seabirds along the shore
whistling their lonesome numbers,
jamming into the small hours
sweet riffs to warm the bones.

Day brings the blackbird's solo,
the Latin singsong of the priest.
I pass hours happily sub-zero,
reclining here in my ivy roost.

It's the old tunes do the trick –
that find the sweet spot of my heart
whether on mountain crag or cliff,
and lift me to the next concert –

psalm-singing at famed Ros Bruic
(though soon to be rechristened)
or the love-call of the young buck
belling from the bare flank of Erc.

Cold my pillow through the long nights
listening to the storming billows,
while songbirds party and jive
in the wildwood of Fid Cuille.

Gusts slamming into the bare oak,
the far off roll and rumble of surf,
ice breaking with a sudden groan –
all to the merry roar of the Rough.

12th c.   MAURICE RIORDAN

58

The Song of Finn in Praise of May

May Day! delightful day!
    Bright colours play the vales along.
Now wakes at morning's slender ray,
    Wild and gay, the blackbird's song.

Now comes the bird of dusty hue,
    The loud cuckoo, the summer-lover;
Branching trees are thick with leaves;
    The bitter, evil time is over.

Swift horses gather nigh
    Where half dry the river goes;
Tufted heather crowns the height;
    Weak and white the bogdown blows.

Corncrake sings from eve till morn,
    Deep in corn, a strenuous bard!
Sings the virgin waterfall,
    White and tall, her one sweet word.

Loaded bees of little power
    Goodly flower-harvest win;
Cattle roam with muddy flanks;
    Busy ants go out and in.

Through the wild harp of the wood
 Making music roars the gale –
Now it slumbers without motion,
 On the ocean sleeps the sail.

Men grow mighty in the May,
 Proud and gay the maidens grow;
Fair is every wooded height;
 Fair and bright the plain below.

A bright shaft has smit the streams,
 With gold gleams the water-flag;
Leaps the fish, and on the hills
 Ardour thrills the flying stag.

Carols loud the lark on high,
 Small and shy, his tireless lay,
Singing in wildest, merriest mood
 Of delicate-hued, delightful May.

?6th/early 7th c. T. W. ROLLESTON

59

[Scél lem dúib]

Here's a song –
stags give tongue
winter snows
summer goes.

High cold blow
sun is low
brief his day
seas give spray.

Fern clumps redden
shapes are hidden
wildgeese raise
wonted cries.

Cold now girds
wings of birds
icy time –
that's my rime.

9th c.   FLANN O'BRIEN

60

Sliabh Cua

cold mountain rough feral black
wolves and winds howl in its glens
howl about its high places
the stag bellows in autumn
in bewilderment of gold
herons sit by its waters

9th c.   THOMAS A. CLARK

61

Gráinne to Finn

There is someone
I would pay dear to gaze on.
I'd give the bright world, all of it,
though it bring me no profit.

10th c.   MAURICE RIORDAN

62

Caílte on Finn

If the brown leaves turned to gold
    when trees let them fall
if silver were the waves' foam
    Finn would give you all

13th c. *Acallam na Senórach*   MAURICE RIORDAN

63

The Praise of Fionn

Patrick you chatter too loud
    And lift your crozier too high,
Your stick would be kindling soon
    If my son Osgar stood by.

If my son Osgar and God
    Wrestled it out on the hill
And I saw Osgar go down
    I'd say that your God fought well.

But how could the God you praise
    And his mild priests singing a tune
Be better than Fionn the swordsman,
    Generous, faultless Fionn?

Just by the strength of their hands
    The Fenians' battles were fought,
With never a spoken lie,
    Never a lie in thought.

There never sat priest in church
    A tuneful psalm to raise
Better spoken than these
    Scarred in a thousand frays.

Whatever your monks have called
    The law of the King of Grace,
That was the Fenians' law;
    His home is their dwelling-place.

If happier house than Heaven
    There be, above or below,
'Tis there my master Fionn
    And his fighting men will go.

Ah, priest, if you saw the Fenians
    Filling the strand beneath
Or gathered in streamy Naas
    You would praise them with every breath.

Patrick, ask of your God
    Does he remember their might,
Or has he seen east or west
    Better men in a fight?

Or known in his own land
    Above the stars and the moon
For wisdom, courage and strength
    A man the like of Fionn?

?16th c.   FRANK O'CONNOR

64

The Sleep-Song of Grainne Over Dermuid
When Fleeing from Fionn

Sleep a little, a little little, thou needest feel no fear or dread,
Youth to whom my love is given, I am watching near thy head.

Sleep a little, with my blessing, Dermuid of the light-some eye,
I will guard thee as thou dreamest, none shall harm while I am by.

Sleep, O little lamb, whose homeland was the country of the lakes,
In whose bosom torrents tremble, from whose sides the
   river breaks.

Sleep as slept the ancient poet, Dedach, minstrel of the South,
When he snatched from Conall Cernach Eithne of the
   laughing mouth.

Sleep as slept the comely Finncha 'neath the falls of Assaroe,
Who, when stately Slaine sought him, laid the Hard-head
   Failbe low.

Sleep in joy, as slept fair Aine, Gailan's daughter of the west,
Where, amid the flaming torches, she and Duvach found
   their rest.

Sleep as Degha, who in triumph, ere the sun sank o'er the land,
Stole the maiden he had craved for, plucked her from fierce
   Deacall's hand.

Fold of Valour, sleep a little, Glory of the Western world;
I am wondering at thy beauty, marvelling how thy locks are curled.

Like the parting of two children, bred together in one home,
Like the breaking of two spirits, if I did not see you come.

Swirl the leaves before the tempest, moans the night-wind o'er
     the lea,
Down its stony bed the streamlet hurries onward to the sea.

In the swaying boughs the linnet twitters in the darkling light,
On the upland wastes of heather wings the grouse its heavy flight.

In the marshland by the river sulks the otter in his den;
While the piping of the peeweet sounds across the distant fen.

On the stormy mere the wild-duck pushes outward from the brake,
With her downy brood beside her seeks the centre of the lake.

In the east the restless roe-deer bellows to his frightened hind;
On thy track the wolf-hounds gather, sniffing up against the wind.

Yet, O Dermuid, sleep a little, this one night our fear hath fled,
Youth to whom my love is given, see, I watch beside thy bed.

17th c./?12th c. *Duanaire Finn*   ELEANOR HULL

65

Arann

island of stags the sea
tapping on its shoulder
an army might feed there
its wits honed in the wind

stags leaping on its crags
cold water in its burns
bilberry blaeberry
oaks heavy with acorns

hounds and hawks for hunting
white blossom on blackthorn
its forests walled by waves
deer dappled in oak shade

lichens gleaned from the shore
webs on dew-drenched grasses
an embroidered cloth
graces dancing in glades

pigs fatten on pasture
you have to believe it
nut harvests on hazel
laden boats find shelter

the days are best when bright
trout pause in the currents
great commotion of gulls
island sharp with delights

13th c. *Acallam na Senórach*   THOMAS A. CLARK

66

The Fort of Árd Ruide

There are three plenties
always in the fort of Árd Ruide:
a plenty of young men, plenty of horses
and a plenty of Mac Lugaid's hunting hounds.

With three sorts of music
sweet for its king to hear:
the harp, the drum echoing,
and the bass of Fer Tuinne Mac Trograin.

There are three calls
heard there always in plenty:
the call of the lamb on the green,
the calls of racing, the call of cattle.

And three other calls:
of black, fat-backed pigs,
of crowds on the palace green,
high company and drink.

There are three harvests
always there on the branches:
a first harvest falling,
a harvest in bloom, and a harvest ripening.

Lugaid left three sons
– where are their riches now?
Ruide, Eochaid, the manly Fiachu,
three sons of Lugaid the Broad.

This I will say for Ruide,
on whom the three plenties fell:
no one ever begged him in vain,
and he never begged from anyone.

This I will say for Eochaid:
he never stepped back in battle
and never told a lie;
none has a finer fame.

And this I will say for Fiachu
– where are his riches now?
He was never long without music
or without a drink of beer . . .

Thirty princes, thirty champions,
thirty chiefs – a king's following:
and the size of his people assembled
three times thirty hundred.

12th c. *Metrical Dindsenchas*   THOMAS KINSELLA

67

Cáel's Praise of the House of Créide

Finn said to Créide 'We have come to choose and woo you.' 'Who has?' asked Créide. 'Cáel son of King Crimthann of Leinster' said Finn. 'We have heard of him,' answered Créide, 'but we haven't seen him. Has he my poem ready for me?' 'Certainly I have' said Cáel, and he stepped forward to recite this:

> As a worthy traveller
> I must risk a Friday journey,
> to Créide's house which faces
> the mountain from North-East.
>
> It is Fortune that has brought me
> to the scenic Paps of Danu
> and the great house of Créide
> for a full week of trial.
>
> Blessed is the house where she dwells
> with men and boys and women,
> with clerics and musicians,
> with butlers and men on guard.
>
> There's an equerry with graces
> and a highly skilful carver:
> all under bidding
> of handsome, fair-haired Créide.

I'll have the greatest luxury
on a fine bed of goose-feathers.
My journey's repaid richly
By Créide's gracious leave.

A bowl filled with juice of berries
holds the dye for her rich mantle.
Sparkling decanters
pour wine for crystal goblets.

Her lime-white skin
lies on quilts upon the rushes.
Silk lines her blue cloak,
and her drinking horn is golden.

Her chamber at Loch Cuire
is plated gold and silver,
roofed with the rarest plumes
of red and brown and purple.

Look at the dark green doorposts
in their well-crafted frames.
The glory of the lintels
is marvelled at by all.

Créide's chair is to the left,
a beauty of all beauties,
standing at her bed's foot
inlaid with Alpine gold.

That bed – the poem's subject –
behind the ornate chair
was made from gold and jewels
by the eastern master Tuile.

On the right another bed
made too of gold and silver,
with a canopy that gleams
with hyacinths carved in bronze.

As for the household,
they were born in an age of gold:
their cloaks not greyed or worn
and their hair of golden lustre.

Wounded, blood-soaked warriors
would sleep sound and happy,
lulled by the haunting birdsong
that rings from the sunstruck eaves.

If I had the grace of Créide
for whom the cuckoo calls,
then I'd compose as many poems
as her bounty grants reward.

If Créide is pleased in this way,
let her hesitate no further
but say to me this instant
'you are welcome to my house'.

That house is a hundred yards
from one gable to the other.
It is twenty yards in breadth
to measure from its threshold.

Its hurdle-roof and thatching
are finished with birds' feathers
of blue and matching yellow.
The wellside shines with crystal.

At every bedstead's corner
are gold and silver bedposts:
each crowned with a shining orb
to give every eye delight.

A red-enamelled trough
stands filled with flowing mead,
shaded by an apple tree
that sheds abundant fruit.

When Créide's horn is filled
with liquor from this source,
four apples fall lightly
straight down to her cup.

All the helpers I have mentioned
start to pour out ale in plenty,
and with the ale an apple
to enrich the other four.

The Creator of everything
from the ebb-tide to the flow
has placed Créide of the mountains
unrivalled past all others.

I've brought here no mere cattle
but a well constructed poem
for Créide the most lovely –
I trust she'll find it pleasing.

13th c. *Acallam na Senórach*   BERNARD O'DONOGHUE

68

Caoilte Laments the Passing of the Fianna

Windswept, untenanted, rises Forad's high hill,
once the look-out of sword-master Fionn;
his war-band has vanished, like the hero himself:
no one hunts now on Allen's wide plain.

The very noblest of households has crumbled,
and who today values high birth?
Illustrious captains who surrounded great Fionn
are ignored now forever in earth.

Roamers over forest and valley, the Fianna
to their deep resting places have gone;
how bitter a fate it is to outlive them
– brave Diarmuid and black-fleeced Conán,

Goll MacMorna from the lowlands of Connaught
and Aillill, whom the hundreds obeyed;
Eogan of the great grey glittering spear
and Conall, ever first into fray.

I mutter their names over and over
and can scarcely believe they are lying,
Dub Drumann among them, covered in clay,
while I am still breathing here, sighing

in grief for my warrior companions
and detesting each minute I live;
I peer out tonight from Fionn's ancient eyrie
and see nothing and no one to love.

13th c. *Acallam na Senórach*   PATRICK CROTTY

69

[Binn guth duine i dTír in Óir]

Clear man's speech in the land of gold
clear the tongues of wing-borne souls
clear the noise the heron makes
clear the breaking of the wave

clear the blowing gale in Autumn
clear the cuckoo's call from Cash Con
bright the fire of the western sun
clear then the blackbird's tune

clear the eagle's shriek at Assaroe
circling above MacMorna's shore
clear the cuckoo hid from sight
bright the heron's arrowed flight

Finn McCool my former lord
led our band in war and sport
when he let slip the hunting dogs
clear their baying along the crags

15th–16th c.   MAURICE RIORDAN

70

The Blackbird of Derrycairn

Stop, stop and listen for the bough top
Is whistling and the sun is brighter
Than God's own shadow in the cup now!
Forget the hour-bell. Mournful matins
Will sound, Patric, as well at nightfall.

Faintly through mist of broken water
Fionn heard my melody in Norway.
He found the forest track, he brought back
This beak to gild the branch and tell, there,
Why men must welcome in the daylight.

He loved the breeze that warns the black grouse,
The shout of gillies in the morning
When packs are counted and the swans cloud
Loch Erne, but more than all those voices
My throat rejoicing from the hawthorn.

In little cells behind a cashel,
Patric, no handbell gives a glad sound.
But knowledge is found among the branches.
Listen! That song that shakes my feathers
Will thong the leather of your satchels.

15th–16th c.   AUSTIN CLARKE

[127]

Notes and Sources

The following poems have been newly translated or revised: 1, 5, 9, 12, 13, 15, 16, 18, 20, 21 (revised), 22 (revised), 25, 34, 35, 36, 39, 40, 41, 42, 44, 46, 48, 49, 50, 52, 57, 60, 61, 62, 65, 67, 68 (revised), 69.

The new translations are based on texts from four main editions:

Gerard Murphy, *Early Irish Lyrics: Eighth to Twelfth Century* (Oxford: Clarendon Press, 1956).

James Carney, *Medieval Irish Lyrics* (Berkeley: University of California Press, 1967).

David Greene & Frank O'Connor, *A Golden Treasury of Irish Poetry AD 600 to 1200* (London: Macmillan, 1967).

Ruth P. M. Lehmann, *Early Irish Verse* (Austin: University of Texas Press, 1982).

The editors' surnames serve as abbreviations. I also give a manuscript source where a poem can be viewed readily online.

1. Murphy, 43. Reichenau Primer, 8 verso top, where it is attributed to 'Suibne geilt' (Sweeney the Wild Man).

2. Murphy, 2. St Gall Priscian Glosses, bottom margins pp. 203–04. Note the insertion of *fidbaide* in the ms:

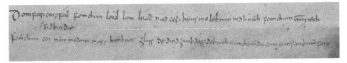

3. Murphy, 1. Reichenau Primer, 1 verso bottom.

4. Greene & O'Connor, 54 (5).

5. Greene & O'Connor, 32. Carney believed this poem to be in accentual metre and of pre-monastic origin. 'Three Old Irish Accentual Poems', *Ériu*, vol 22 (1971), pp. 23–80.

6. 'The Guesting of Aithirne', edited by Kuno Meyer. *Ériu,* vol 7 (1914), pp. 1–9. Translation is from the introduction to Greene & O'Connor, p. 13.

7. Carney, 22. St Gall Priscian Glosses, top margin, p. 112.

8. Greene & O'Connor, 54 (1).

9. Greene & O'Connor, 29.

10. Greene & O'Connor, 54 (2).

11. Greene & O'Connor, 54 (4).

12. Greene & O'Connor, 54 (3). Written across top margin of page 36 in *An Leabhar Breac* (The Speckled Book).

13. Lehmann, 5. The Book of Leinster, top margin fac 356.

14. Translated for Samuel Barber's cycle of *Hermit Songs* (1953). The manuscript is in Harleian 5280, top margin p. 227, as noted by Kuno Meyer, 'Anecdota from Irish Ms', *The Gaelic Journal,* vol IV (1889), p. 115.

15. Murphy, 12.

16. Murphy, 9.

17. Murphy, 3.

18. Murphy, 17.

19. Greene & O'Connor, 42.

20. Murphy, 8.

21. Greene & O'Connor, 2.

22. Murphy, 11.

23. Greene & O'Connor, 11.

24. Translation from the introduction to Greene & O'Connor, p. 11.

25. Translation based on Donncha Ó hAodha's edition of the text, 'The Lament of the Old Woman of Beare', in Donnchadh Ó Corráin, Liam Breatnach and Kim McCone (eds), *Sages, Saints and Storytellers: Celtic Studies in Honour of Professor James Carney* (Maynooth Monographs 2. Maynooth: An Sagart, 1989), pp. 308–31.

26. Murphy, 21.

27. Murphy, 35.

28. Murphy, 36.

29. Carney, 28.

30. Free version of a textually problematic poem in *Longes mac nUislenn* (The Exile of the Sons of Ulster).

COLM CILLE

31–36. Colm Cille, also known as St Columba (521–597), has close associations with Derry, where he founded a monastery. He left Ireland in 563 and established a monastic community on Iona. He became a semi-mythic figure who attracted many legends. In the 11th and 12th centuries numerous poems were attributed to him.

31. Beccán was a member of the Iona community and he is thought to have composed this poem around 640.

32. Murphy, 29.

33. Murphy, 32.

34. Lehmann, 41.

35. Murphy, 30.

36. Murphy, 33.

37. Lehmann, 36.

39. Kuno Meyer, *Zeitschrift für Celtische Philologie*, vol VIII (1912), p. 175. Cassiodorus's Commentary on the Psalms, Laon, top margin, f 15r.

40. Murphy, 38. An example of *debide baise fri tóin*, which translates as 'slap-on-the-bottom verse', or more loosely 'kick-arse verse'.

41. Greene & O'Connor, 26 (1).

42. Carney, 80. Codex Boernerianus, f 23v, bottom margin.

43. Kuno Meyer, *A Primer of Irish Metrics* (Dublin: Hodges, Figgis; London: David Nutt, 1909), p. 24.

44. Lehmann, 95.

45. Lehmann, 98.

46. Carney, 62. Extracted from a lengthy topographical work in Rawlinson B 502, 45r.

47. Murphy, 41.

48. Murphy, 42. From 'The Wasting Sickness of Cu Chulainn', in *Lebor na hUidre* (The Book of the Dun Cow), f 48a.

49. Murphy, 39.

50. Murphy, 40. From The Voyage of Mael Duin.

51. Based on P. W. Joyce's *Old Celtic Romances* (1879).

52. *Aislinge Meic Conglinne: The Vision of Mac Conglinne,* edited by Lahney Preston-Matto (Syracuse: Syracuse University Press, 2010).

SWEENEY THE WILD MAN

Suibne Geilt (Sweeney the Madman) was a historical king who, according to legend, went mad at the Battle of Mag Rath in 639 CE. In the tale, he is married to Éorann. He quarrels with St Ronan, who curses him. As a result he begins to fly in the course of the battle and thereafter he lives in the woods. Near the end of the tale, and his life, he is befriended and taken in from the wilderness by St Moling. The main extant work is *Buile Suibne,* a 12th-century romance.

53–56. *The Adventures of Suibhne Geilt* (1913). Edited and translated by J. G. O'Keefe (Dublin: Irish Texts Society, 1913).

57. Murphy, 44. I follow Murphy's suggestion that the poem may end at stanza 10.

THE FINN CYCLE

According to tradition, the legendary Finn mac Cumhaill and his band of warriors and huntsmen, the Fianna, flourished during the reign of Cormac mac Airt in the third century. Poetry and stories relating to their exploits are recorded from the seventh century. Fenian lore attained its greatest popularity around 1200. It remained a vital part of Irish and Scottish folklore until recent times. See Introduction, pp. xxviii–xxx.

58. Murphy, 52. Carney re-edited this poem, 'Three Old Accentual Irish Poems', *Ériu*, vol 22 (1971), pp. 41–3. See Introduction, p. xxvi.

59. Murphy, 53.

60. Lehmann, 14.

61. Murphy, 54. Rawlinson B 502, f 56r, col. 2, l. 28.

62. Lehmann, 75.

64. *Duanaire Finn: The Book of the Lays of Fionn,* part I, edited and translated by Eoin MacNeill (London: Alfred Nutt, 1908). Gerard Murphy restored this poem to its 12th-century 'original'. See Introduction, pp. xxvii–xxviii.

65. Lehmann, 76.

66. *The Metrical Dindshenchas,* vol. 4, edited and translated by Edward Gwynn (Dublin: Hodges, Figgis, 1924), 368.

67. Murphy, 48

68. Murphy, 50.

69. Lehmann, 85. From The Book of the Dean of Lismore (Scottish).

70. Based on '*Lon duire an choirn*', *Measgra Dánta: Miscellaneous Irish Poems* vol I, edited by Thomas F. O'Rahilly (Dublin and Cork: Cork University Press, 1927), 37.

Acknowledgements

My thanks are due above all to the translators who contribute to this anthology. I am especially grateful to the poets who have written new translations: Ciaran Carson, Thomas A. Clark, Patrick Crotty, Greg Delanty, Kathleen Jamie, Paul Muldoon, Eiléan Ní Chuilleanáin, Bernard O'Donoghue, Christopher Reid. I was further indebted to Seamus Heaney for giving me a folder of his uncollected translations. Particular acknowledgement is due to Paul Keegan, whose brainchild the book was; and I'd like to thank Matthew Hollis and Martha Sprackland for their diligence in ensuring it has come to completion. I am grateful for a period of leave from Sheffield Hallam University that enabled me to concentrate on the work. Patrick Crotty generously offered me his suggestions and advice on numerous matters throughout. Specific thanks are due to Professor Liam Breatnach for help with the editorial history of *Domfarcai fidbaide fál*. Kathryn Maris has been unfaltering in her support and advice. Finally, I want to thank John Montague, who first stirred my interest in early Irish poetry when I was a student.

M.R.

[136]

Index of Titles and First Lines